The Complete Chondro: A comprehensive guide to the care and breeding of Green Tree Pythons
by Greg Maxwell

© 2003 ECO Publishing / Greg Maxwell

ISBN 0-9713197-4-X

No part of this book can be reproduced or utilized in any form or by any means, electronic or mechanical, including photocopying, recording, or by any information storage or retrieval systems, without permission in writing from the publisher.

Published by ECO Publishing in cooperation with Zoo Book Sales.
Printed in China.

Copies available from:
ECO Publishing
915 Seymour
Lansing, MI 48906 USA

telephone: 517.487.5595   fax: 517.371.2709
email: ecoorders@hotmail.com
website: http://www.reptileshirts.com

All photos by the author unless otherwise acknowledged.

Design and layout by Russ Gurley.

Cover design by Bob Ashley and Greg Maxwell.

Cover background photo: Cape York Peninsula, Australia by Bob Ashley. Cover Green Tree Python photo: Female produced by the author in 2000 traces her ancestry to both the first zoo breeding of *Morelia viridis* in the U.S. as well as the first private breeding.

Title page photo: "Aquagirl" (TW-93-12).

Front endpaper: "Rosina" (TW-98-26).

Rear endpaper: "Zulu", produced by Alan Zulich in 1995.

The Complete Chondro

A comprehensive guide to the care and breeding of Green Tree Pythons

Greg Maxwell

Table of Contents

Foreword i

Acknowledgements iv

Introduction 1

Section I. Meet the Green Tree Python

Chapter 1. Natural History 6

Chapter 2. Captive History 18

Chapter 3. Geographic Races and Locality Typing . 31

Chapter 4. Color and Pattern Morphs and Genetics . 51

Chapter 5. Chondro Myths and Misunderstandings . 95

Section II. Captive Husbandry

Chapter 6. Are Chondros Right For You? . . 102

Chapter 7. Buying A Quality Chondro . . . 113

Chapter 8. Proper Caging 122

Chapter 9. Providing Proper Cage Environment . . 140

Chapter 10. Feeding, Defecation, and Shedding Cycles . 159

Section III. Captive Breeding

Chapter 11. The Challenge of Breeding Chondros . 176

Chapter 12. Conditioning and Cycling . . . 181

Chapter 13. Breeding and Egg Laying . . . 188

Chapter 14. Incubation 203

Chapter 15. Managing Neonates . . . 222

Appendix A. Solving Common Problems . . 234

Appendix B. Resources 242

Appendix C. Common Medical Dosages . . 244

Suggested Reading 246

Foreword

The day I met Greg Maxwell I knew in my spirit that there was something "different" about this fellow, and that he was to play an important role in the future of captive bred Chondros, and my retirement fund...

No, no, noooooo. Let me start over...

When Greg Maxwell asked me to write the foreward for his new book, *The Complete Chondro*, many thoughts came to mind, including a flood of memories of how and when we first met. Actually, I had forgotten how we met...so I asked him – then the flood came.

It seems we had our first chance encounter at the Reptile Breeders Expo in 1993, which was then held in Orlando, Florida. Greg and I were both vendors at the show. At the time I was a Biologist at the Smithsonian National Zoo by day, and a private Chondro breeder/owner/lover first and foremost. Greg was representing his reptile cage business, CageMaster, and I was working the tables of Ophiological Services (OS) with owner, Gene Bessette. For many years I had worked with OS in the pursuit of understanding the Green Tree Python, (then known as *Chondropython viridis*), and in providing a regular source of quality, captive born "chondros" backed up with excellent after sales service, surpassed by none. Our motto for the show that year was **"Buy the Best, Forget the Rest...!"**. Gene had set me up with an entire table *stacked* with our baby and yearling chondros – some of the finest Designer specimens (also referred to as "TW Basement Mutts") available at that time anywhere in the world. To say that Greg Maxwell was bitten by the Chondro bug at the Expo that day is a vast understatement!

Fact is Greg and I really met for the first time several months later at another reptile show in Richmond, Virginia. Again, Greg was awestruck, but on this occasion we had more time to speak about his interests. The conversation went something like this...

GM – "I've absolutely got to have some of them!" TW- "Show me your wallet, young man!!"

It so happened Greg had a huge wad of cash from a very successful show's earnings at the CageMaster tables. TW- "Hmmmm. I'll tell you what… Have I got a deal for you…?…!! If you buy **20** of my Designer Chondros, I will give you the next one **FREE…!!**" I went on to explain to Greg the difference between captive bred chondros and wild caught specimens, which at the time were few and far between, but worlds apart in terms of the care necessary to help them thrive in captivity. I showed Greg cage cards on the snakes I had on offer at the show as well as examples of my chondro pedigrees, which even then went back four and five generations. I explained how chondros had become the first highly specialized, exotic snake to become "domesticated" in captivity. We discussed some of the many special elements common to Chondros…the brilliant colors of young and adult animals…the incredible ontogenic color morphing process and differences in same between red and yellow babies… Greg's eyes were now wide open, although his wallet was not.

Greg mentioned he had a lot of experience working with boas and pythons, and how he had successfully bred a variety of colubrids over the years. I explained how you could be a successful <u>python</u> breeder, and yet not be a competent <u>green tree</u> python breeder. Becoming a successful chondro farmer, producing these gems on a consistent basis over a long period of time, requires a passion, and the ability to learn a new (snake) language (chondro), plus an *enormous* amount of patience…and not necessarily in that order. Did I mention patience? And passion? Yeah, lots of both!! I told him how, gram for gram, chondros are a better investment than gold to someone who can breed them consistently, and is willing to share their Chondro Passion with others.

At the end of the show Greg returned with two of his friends, Phil Black and Marc "Seig" Seymour. Actually, Greg was being supported on either side by his friends, and he was trembling uncontrollably while sweating profusely. In his right hand he held tight to a wad of cash, the exact amount I had been asking for a particularly gorgeous red baby. "I must have…the snake. Must have…" I smiled to myself. I knew he was mine. And later on, so were his friends, Phil and Marc.

Over the next ten years Greg subsidized my family income through purchasing virtually all of the finest chondros I could produce, including the now famous "Computer Chondro" that has become the centerpiece of his collection, and which now consists of only chondros. Two years ago Greg earned his freebie 21st chondro and is now working on the next 20. Greg proved to be an avid learner, speaking fluent chondro within his second year and producing his first babies soon after. Passion speaks louder than words and Greg's is loud indeed. The student has become the teacher, and he has done very well with his animals by all standards.

Today Greg Maxwell maintains what I believe to be one of the best reptile web sites on the net, and in fact *the* most *complete* chondro web site in existence. Passion is also contagious and Greg's passion is now shared by other new "Chondroheads", many of whom started off as his early customers but have grown to be good friends.

I am honored to be one of the first people to read Greg Maxwell's book, *The Complete Chondro*, and even more honored that he would ask me to write the Foreword. This popular-style book fills the gap in the existing literature at a time when Chondromania is at an all-time high. *The Complete Chondro* takes you step-by-step through the entire process of Chondro-Rewards… beginning with a dissertation on the responsibilities of Chondro ownership, and on to purchasing your first animal…then into all the how-to information of husbandry and breeding which chondro keepers are likely to need. The photos **ALONE** are an incredible teaching tool, for Chondro-Newbies and Chondro-Old-Farts alike. Chondro passion is alive and well… and growing. I dare you to read this book and not be impressed! Even if you never own a chondro! But chances are if you have just read this Foreword, you will own chondros. Or do they own you? And, remember – you *can't* own just one…

Think Green… and Yellow… and Blue… and White… and Green/Yellow/Blue/White, and most of all – enjoy…!…TW<<

Trooper Walsh
DragonTails

Acknowledgements

There are many individuals who have helped make this book a reality, as well as several persons who have had an important influence on me. This latter group includes Trooper Walsh for his pioneering work with chondros, as well as his friendship and infectious attention to details; Al Zulich for teaching me how to feed neonate chondros; Philip Black for his long friendship that includes having helped me lug at least 1.5 tons of cages around the eastern U.S., for helping greatly with my evolution as a writer, and for the innumerable ways he has inspired and encouraged me; Thomas Phillips for his friendship, enthusiasm for chondros, teaching me web design (including many hours on the phone telling me why what I just did isn't working!), help with proof reading the text and making valuable suggestions, and for his balance and leadership as a ChondroForum co-Administrator; and Thomas Tucker, my long time friend and pastor who has always encouraged me to be my best and to use the God-given gifts I have been given, even when that meant that I could not be as involved with church activities as he would like. Special thanks are due to Kim Heller and Terri Edwards, not only for their friendship and support, but also for shouldering much of my Forum administrative duties during my writing sabbatical. Thanks to Damon Salceies, Steve Gordon, Marcial Mendez, John Holland, Chris Rouille, and Janet Hickner for supplying additional photos. Special thanks go to Mark O'Shea for supplying habitat photos and reviewing the chapter on natural history.

There is not enough space to mention each person who has become a good friend, or has in some way inspired or encouraged me, but you all know who you are, and you are greatly appreciated. In fact, I owe the entire community of Green Tree Python lovers a big "thanks" for the enthusiasm they show for chondros, and for the contributions many of them have made to our body of knowledge about these animals. I also owe a huge debt of gratitude to my parents, who not only encouraged my naturalist pursuits, but also permitted me to house large collections of herps in their home. Finally, I need to express the extreme gratitude and love that I feel for Grace, my wife of twenty-something years, and for my children

Gideon, Dan, and Melody. All of them have contributed in innumerable ways, not only to this project, but also to my being able to work with reptiles for a living. Without their cooperation, support, understanding, and tolerance, this book would not have been written, and I would not be the person I am today. Therefore, I dedicate this book to them.

Introduction

Welcome to the world of the Green Tree Python (*Morelia viridis*), that beautiful and mysterious inhabitant of the New Guinea and northern Australia rain forests. This nocturnal, tree-dwelling serpent is truly one of God's special creatures, and has been a major source of fascination and wonder in my life.

In this book, I will introduce you to the Green Tree Python (GTP), or "chondro", the nickname given them by those who know and love them as captives. We will cover everything from the geography and climate of the chondro's wild home, to providing the best captive environment and breeding conditions. We'll talk about solving common problems associated with captive tree pythons, and discuss the ethics of keeping and breeding.

As interest in keeping and breeding GTPs has steadily increased over the last ten years or so, a definite need has developed to take the body of work, experience, and efforts of successful keepers and breeders, and put them into one volume for the chondro community to use as a reference. I feel there is also a need to sort out fact from fiction regarding this often mysterious and controversial species. I have applied over thirty years worth of reptile husbandry and breeding experience to working with chondros, and they have become one of my life's passions. I now keep and breed them exclusively.

There are many issues dealing with the captive husbandry and reproduction of Green Tree Pythons that are controversial in nature, and many different opinions exist. Many people, including the author, are passionate about which conclusions are the correct ones! We can't even agree on the scientific name, for crying out loud! (The time-honored *Chondropython* genus, which is where "chondros" get their slang name, was changed some time ago to *Morelia*, much to the irritation and dismay of some chondro fans. More will be said about this in Chapter 1.) The information and views expressed in this book are based on years of hands-on experience and observation, and most are further backed up by the collective experiences of veteran keepers and Green Tree Python pioneers.

The title "The Complete Chondro" refers to my attempt to include everything I have learned about these snakes, and to provide a full-service resource for keepers and breeders. I hope it does not suggest that there is nothing more to learn! The late herpetologist Carl Kauffeld once observed that a specialist is one who "learns more and more about less and less". Since deciding to focus exclusively on keeping and breeding chondros several years ago, it seems to me that the more we learn about them, the less we do know. For example, we have just begun to scratch the surface of deciphering the mysteries of ontogenic color changes, or the genetic trait functions associated with neonates and unusually colored adult specimens. But, I hope that this volume will serve as a springboard for future discoveries, while covering the fundamentals about which we now have some depth of understanding. I will do my best to include the viewpoints of those whose perspectives differ from my own, so long as they fall within the realm of good critical thinking, and have some logic to them. I'll also attempt to identify those conclusions that are strictly my opinion, and separate them from those that are established and accepted facts.

I have decided to include the popular nicknames given to many of the individual chondros referred to in the text or shown in the photographs. I realize that some readers may not be fond of giving such names to animals, and I do think that some reptile owners tend toward anthropomorphism (the attribution of human characteristics to animals). However, it has become apparent that many chondro lovers can more easily relate to a name than they can to an ID number assigned to an animal. We see this same principle at work with thoroughbred horses and show dogs. Since a growing number of valuable breeder chondros are known in the breeding and collecting community by their popular names, it seems appropriate to include the names here. For example, "Calico Junior" calls to mind the specific animal referred to, much more readily than # GM-99-09. This is a recognized trade name for the animal and his bloodline, much like "Secretariat" is to the racing horse community. I hope that the reader will understand that this is different than simply calling one of my pets "Mr. Squiggles" or "Monty Python". To hedge all bets, I have included the pedigree ascension ID number in parenthesis following popular names, when this is known. It may surprise a few readers to learn than many serious chondro breeders keep bloodline pedigrees on their animals, and refer to breeders as "sire" and "dam". This helps build heritage and credibility within the breeder's program, as well as communicating the level of commitment to quality and value that such breeders have. I have adopted the ID code format suggested by several people as the best and most intuitive: The breeder's initials (GM) followed by the year the animal hatched (99) and then the individual animal's number (09). This last number usually indicates the hatch order for a given year; i.e. "09" means the animal was the 9th hatchling that year.

It is my fervent hope that this book does more than teach the basic principles of GTP care and captive reproduction. I also hope to instill in my readers the same sense of awe for these remarkable snakes that I have; to communicate the same sense of responsibility for ethical husbandry and breeding practices that were taught to me by those who introduced me to chondros; and to convince you of the responsibility we all share for helping to maintain the integrity and value of the species commercially. I make no apology for engaging in such moralizing. In my opinion the wonderful privilege of owning these denizens of the rain forest carries with it responsibilities no less than these. As Ralph Waldo Emerson said, *"All high beauty has a moral element in it"*.

Greg Maxwell
Mt. Vernon, Ohio USA

About the Photography

All the photographs in this book, except where noted, were taken by the author using a Nikon Coolpix 990 digital camera. Lighting for the numerous portrait photos was supplied by two Smith-Victor® 600 watt, 3200K DYH quartz lamps with white bounce umbrellas. Two 100-watt GE Reveal® full-spectrum incandescent bulbs provided additional foreground lighting. Ambient overhead lighting was supplied by two 48" GE fluorescent Kitchen and Bath® bulbs. Most shots were taken using manual mode, white balance preset.

Calico Junior (GM-99-09) and Chiquita (GM-99-01) get chummy for the camera.

Section I. Meet the Green Tree Python

This is not a trick photograph, just a chondro being a chondro.

Chapter 1. The Natural History of the Green Tree Python

"Everything on Earth is beautiful, everything, except what we ourselves think and do when we forget the higher purposes of life and our own human dignity."

Anton Chekhov

The Green Tree Python, (*Morelia viridis*), is a very beautiful, arboreal (tree-dwelling), nocturnal (active at night), python from the rain forests of New Guinea and some of the surrounding islands that are part of Indonesia. It is also found on the Cape York Peninsula of Northern Australia. While the main focus of this book is on GTPs in captivity, it is my belief that learning a little about the geography and climate of the native habitat of these small pythons helps keepers to provide a better environment for them in captive settings, as well as adds to the overall enjoyment of keeping them.

Habitat and Climate

The habitat of the chondro is wild, remote, diverse, and gorgeous, with varied terrain and landscape. The island of New Guinea is equatorial in location, which means that much of it is hot, humid, and has a high annual amount of rainfall. It has the second largest tract of tropical rainforest left in the world - only the Amazon has more. New Guinea averages at least 80 inches of rainfall per year in the lower elevations and over 120 inches in the mountainous regions. Daily maximum rainfall amounts can be extremely high, with several locations having recorded between 20 and 28 inches. The year is divided between the wet and dry seasons, and these vary in length and intensity depending on location and elevation. Only the Lesser Sunda Islands and Eastern Java have a well-developed dry season.

Locations on the equator and far from the tempering dry air from the Australian landmass have little or no dry season, but enjoy lower amounts of rain during several months. New Guinea's location between the landmasses of Australia and Asia makes it subject to their strong influences on the Monsoon rainfall patterns. The wet season extends from November through April, and the dry season from May through October,

Laloki River, above Port Moresby (Central Province, PNG): heavily forested gorge. Photo courtesy of Mark O'Shea.

but these are rough timeframes and there is great variation, with most of the area receiving heavy precipitation most of the year. Strong afternoon thunderstorms are common. It is no coincidence that many captive breeders report breeding activity during strong low-pressure systems accompanying rainy periods.

Ambua (Southern Highlands Province, PNG): primary montane rainforest. Photo courtesy of Mark O'Shea.

With all that rain, it comes as no surprise that the average relative humidity is high year round; or about 80%. Temperatures are high too, with the warmest average daily temperatures recorded in the coastal areas and moderating somewhat in the higher elevations. Temperatures generally range from a low of 68° F to a high of 89° F. Temperature extremes for Jakarta, a city on the Island of Java that is roughly the same latitude as the Aru Islands (location of one of the GTP populations), range from an all time high of 99° F to a record low of 66° F. Temperatures can drop even lower in the mountains. Average temperatures don't vary much from summer to winter, and the photoperiod (the number of hours of daylight during each 24-hour period) is also consistent, owing to the location near the equator. This means that there are about 12 hours of daylight and 12 hours of darkness year round.

Oriomo (Western Province, PNG): monsoon forest over tidal mud-flats. Photo courtesy of Mark O'Shea.

This information leads to the logical conclusion that chondros in captivity do best with a cage environment that is relatively high in humidity, warm (78 to 88° F), and with each 24-hour period roughly divided between twelve hours of light and twelve hours of darkness. As we will discuss in detail later, it is also prudent to provide fluctuations in both temperature and humidity during each 24-hour cycle.

Not much is known about the habits of GTPs in the wild. Tidbits of knowledge are gained from the field observations made by collectors, park rangers, and naturalists who have had the opportunity to see the chondro in its native habitat. As their common name implies, GTPs do spend most of their time off the ground. Switak reports collecting a specimen discovered fifteen feet high in a tree. However, many observers indicate that they are not always dwellers of the rain forest canopy, being found much more frequently in low scrub cover. Unlike the

Alexishafen (Madag Province, PNG): Secondary forest on old WWII Japanese airstrip. Such overgrown, formerly cleared areas provide both transition habitat for reptiles and their prey, and access for humans. Photo courtesy of Mark O'Shea.

similarly colored Emerald Tree Boa from South America, that moves like a "fish out of water" when not perched on a branch, chondros seem quite comfortable on the ground. This fact surprises a lot of GTP owners, who frequently take alarm if one of their animals chooses to spend a day or two resting on the floor of the cage. Several importers have remarked that local natives collect many wild GTPs as they crawl across roads at night. It may be that some specimens favor more elevated habitats that are less accessible to humans, and so give the impression that specimens found in low habitats represent the norm. At the very least, we know that *Morelia viridis* isn't afraid to descend and to utilize habitat close to the ground. As mentioned, captive specimens often rest on the ground, and more will be said about this later.

It is often reported that GTPs are locally abundant in the areas where proper habitat is in close proximity to human activity and habitation. In fact, many of the so-called "locality" names for these animals are taken from collecting locations near to airports, which helps to simplify exportation. Chondros reportedly range from sea level up to elevations of just over 6500 feet (2000 meters). It stands to reason that these beautiful pythons probably occur in large numbers anywhere that suitable habitat

Spraying cages daily is part of a good husbandry regimen, and helps provide adequate humidity and hydration.

and abundant food supplies can be found. Since much of their wild range is rugged and uninhabited, there is still a lot of data to be gathered and analyzed. At the time of this writing, political unrest in parts of Indonesia has made fieldwork dangerous in some areas of West Papua (formerly Irian Jaya).

Taxonomy

And now, what about that name? As I mentioned in the introduction, chondros haven't always belonged to the genus *Morelia*. For over one hundred years they were known as *Chondropython*, and many of those who have worked with this species a long time have a certain affection for this name. After all, we call them "chondros" and always will. The unusual name *Chondropython*, with this single species making up the genus, just seems to suit these unique serpents, and some of us didn't really see a need to mess with that! Why the change, especially when every scientist and snake lover in the world recognized *Chondropython*? The answer lies in the deeper purposes of scientific nomenclature.

Schlegel described the distinct genus in 1872, based on the mistaken

Many chondros like to hide on the cage flooring among the plants. Can you spot this chondro in its resting place?

belief that the snakes lacked premaxillary teeth. He used the name *Chondropython viridis* to identify them. These two words translate as "cartilage or granular", and "green", respectively; in other words, "granular green python". It is speculated that Schlegel may have used the term to refer to the granular appearance of the tiny head scales, or perhaps the appearance of the large head lobes. McDowell questioned the validity of *Chondropython* in 1975, and in 1994, a paper written by Arnold Kluge sealed the fate of the old name (Barker, pers. com.). *Chondropython* was eliminated, and the snakes were reassigned to the genus *Morelia*, to reflect a close relationship with that group of pythons, of which the Carpet Python (*Morelia spilota*) is probably the best known. This change in how we identify the Green Tree Python illustrates that, along with providing a universal language for reference and communication within the world wide scientific community, the language must also reflect the blood relationships of organisms, to the best of our current understanding.

In a world where very little seems secure and reliable, perhaps some of us can be forgiven for wanting to hang on to something old and familiar. That's why the snakes in my house will always be referred to as "Chondros"!

Biology

GTPs are small, as pythons go. Even a large adult is smaller in girth than the average person's wrist. The author has observed specimens over six feet in length and approaching 2000 grams in weight, but these are exceptional. The average adult male will be between four and five feet in length, and will weigh 900 to 1200 grams. Average females are a bit larger, and a few really big specimens can weigh over 2000 grams (Worrell, pers. com.). The average adult female in the author's collection weighs about 1200-1500 grams prior to cycling for breeding. An experienced person can sometimes predict the sex of yearling animals, based on the smaller size and more streamlined body shape of the males. Animals from Biak Island are usually reported to be the largest of the geographic races, but a specimen of apparent Aru ancestry is the largest ever personally observed by the author.

Chondros can be fairly long-lived in captivity. Current data from most private breeders indicates that males out live females, and there is a documented case of one male living to over twenty years of age at the Smithsonian National Zoo in Washington, D.C. (Walsh, pers. com. 2001). Slavens reports that a wild caught female lived twenty years, seven

"Beauty", a large Aru-type female that exceeds six feet in length. This is larger than the average adult chondro. Animal courtesy of Thomas Phillips.

months at the Brookfield Zoo. Longevity records of animals over ten years of age are becoming common, and it seems reasonable to expect animals of both sexes to reach an age of fifteen years or more with proper care. "Proper care" includes using prudence in the determination of female cycling and breeding regimens, as the toll on females from fasting and egg production can be substantial. Indeed, most female deaths in captivity seem related to complications arising from reproduction, rather than from old age or disease.

GTPs share some characteristics with most other kinds of snakes. Being exothermic ("cold blooded"), they are reliant on their surrounding environment for temperature regulation, and like most reptiles they are highly skilled at thermoregulation. This is the ability to micro-manage their body temperature using small variables in their habitat. This can be seen to an extreme in some types of snakes inhabiting northern latitudes, which have been observed to be active with snow cover still visible in places. Obviously these specimens have body temperatures higher than 32° F. Chondros have all the same internal organs common to most vertebrates, including heart, stomach, liver, gall bladder, intestines, and two lungs (a larger one and a smaller one). The tongue is used in the same manner as other snakes, to sample and analyze spoors from the environment.

GTPs are nocturnal by nature, resting quietly on a chosen perch during daylight hours, and actively taking up prowling and hunting as dusk descends. Like other nocturnal species, they have elliptical ("cat") pupils that provide them with excellent nighttime vision. If captive specimens are any indication, the animals may utilize a favorite resting spot day after day, returning to it after a night's hunting. No doubt the selection of such a place corresponds to desired environmental factors including temperature and security. If food is plentiful, the animals may simply take up a characteristic ambush posture, with the head and several inches of the neck hanging down from the perch. The neck is loosely curved into an "s", preparatory to striking. Even the tamest captive specimens are on high alert when observed in this nocturnal hunting posture, and they will strike at the slightest movement. Chondros seem to be the most active during the first two hours or so of darkness.

Like other boids, GTPs have heat sensitive labial pits. These can accurately detect minute changes in temperature and are useful in locating and overcoming warm-blooded prey. That chondros rely heavily on these thermo-sensing pits is evidenced by the fact that recalcitrant feeders can often be induced to strike prey after it has been warmed. The snakes will also frequently strike at the human hand if it is within range, while food is

This nighttime photo shows the typical head-down ambush position that most chondros assume as dusk descends.

being offered, indicating that heat is as much a cue for the feeding response as scent is.

Chondros also have cloacal spurs, as do other boid species. These are often larger in mature males, and small or lacking in females, but spur size alone is not a reliable sex indicator. Males often use their spurs to tickle and titillate females during courtship.

Chondros also have some characteristics that distinguish them from many other species. Unlike most other boids, chondros are arboreal, spending most of the time off the ground and perched in trees or scrub growth. They have more slender bodies compared to most other pythons, and they are well suited to life above ground, in the growth of the rain forest. Further enabling this aerial existence is the prehensile tail, an appendage that is able to grip and cling to objects.

Chondros can show an amazing ability to maintain their grip on perches, tub rims, plants… anything within reach of the tail. They can sometimes be observed curling the tail in reverse while moving the posterior part of the body in a backwards direction, almost as if they were winching

Heat sensitive pits are found in certain of the labial scales of GTPs. It has been speculated that brooding females may even use these pits to help thermoregulate their eggs.

themselves back to the security of the perch. As was mentioned earlier in this chapter, chondros are not hesitant to leave an elevated perch, and may prowl or even rest on the ground. Unlike the Emerald Tree Boa, *Corallus caninus*, which acts uncomfortable and awkward when not on a perch and which I have never observed resting on a cage floor, chondros seem very confident on the ground.

Chondros have a very fascinating use for their prehensile tail that captivates owners new and old - the practice of caudal luring. This behavior is most often seen in the animals as dusk approaches, and is quite entertaining to watch. The last few inches of the tail is held erect, and a very lifelike imitation of a small worm or caterpillar

Spurs on a male chondro can be quite long. The presence or absence of spurs is not a reliable indicator of gender.

15

Chondros are skilled at gripping a perch with their prehensile tails and it can be difficult to convince them to release.

is effected by the twitching, wiggling, and curling and uncurling of the appendage. When watching this, it is extremely easy to imagine how a frog, lizard, bird, or any other animal that would fancy a tender meal of small insect would be fooled into making a grab for the tail. Many keepers assume that the chondros "know" what they are doing when caudal luring and are "asking" for food when showing the behavior. It is very true that chondros seem in possession of more intelligence than most snakes and can react and relate with keepers in ways other species don't seem capable of. However, I believe that caudal luring is an instinctive, and often subconscious, behavior that the animals engage in out of nervousness or excitement, as well as hunger. Chondros will often begin luring at the sight of a human approaching them in the evening and this has led to the conclusion they are begging for food, like a dog. GTPs may be one of the more intelligent of reptile species, but they aren't that smart! I have seen caudal luring in angry, non-feeding animals, and even disturbed gravid females that were solidly off feed. I think the behavior is a deep-rooted, instinctive reaction to certain exciting stimuli that may have some benefits to the animal when

This female is on high alert and is exhibiting caudal luring behavior. Caution must be exercised because such specimens will often strike at the slightest warmth or movement.

observed by potential prey, rather than a conscious deliberate act.

Wild specimens have a well-deserved reputation for being snappy and a few captive bred individuals can also be ill tempered, but truly savage ones are the exception. The average captive bred adult will respond well to gentle handling and patience, and the majority can safely be handled during the day. As a species, GTPs are somewhat delicate and nervous compared to many other types of boids and are easily stressed from excessive handling. It is best to go easy with individual specimens at first and gradually acclimate them to handling. Some chondros will not tolerate this well and are best observed without being forced to accept interaction with humans.

In this quick overview of GTP habitat and natural history, we have gained a glimpse into their world. In the next chapter, we will begin looking at how chondros have been brought into ours.

Chapter 2. A Brief Captive History of the Green Tree Python

"Any written history inevitably reflects the thought of the author in his time and cultural setting."

Charles A. Beard

As the title of this chapter implies, the information presented here is not intended to be exhaustive and is included to provide a basic understanding of the history of the work with *Morelia viridis*, primarily that which has gone on in the private sector in the United States. It should be noted that there are many dedicated GTP enthusiasts and breeders in Europe and other countries and that some of their work with the species predates what has taken place in the United States. Nevertheless, there has been an enormous swell of interest directed at chondros in this country for the last twenty years or so, and there is no doubt that private American breeders are producing the majority of captive bred chondros in the world today. The U.S. breeders are leading the way in the development and production of so-called "designer morphs" of chondros, including high yellow, high blue, calico, "mite phase", and other selectively bred colors and patterns. Therefore, it seems appropriate to discuss a little of the history of the work with these pythons in captivity in the U.S. It has always been my belief that some knowledge about the work that laid the foundation for the current popularity of chondros helps to build a heritage that adds to the enjoyment and value of working with them today.

The Early Years

The first hatching of GTP babies in captivity in the United States occurred on October 4, 1973 under the supervision of Karl Switak, at the Steinhart Aquarium in San Francisco, CA. Switak was bringing a gravid wild caught female *Chondropython* back to the U.S. from a field trip to New Guinea when she laid eggs in the bag containing her, en route to home. Some of the eggs hatched successfully and history was made. Switak chronicled the story of his travels in a two-part article for Reptiles Magazine in 1995, and the episode with the gravid female and the first captive hatch has become a part of chondro folklore.

This beautiful blue female "Alice" (GM-99-42), produced in 1999 by the author, is a fifth-generation CB offspring from the original WC female captured gravid by Switak in 1973.

Three years later, in October of 1976, the Sedgewick County Zoo in Wichita, Kansas hatched the first clutch of captive bred GTPs in the United States. Also at this time, a young private breeder named Trooper Walsh was accumulating a collection of imported chondros, and also managed to acquire specimens from the 1973 and 1976 clutches. Walsh achieved his own breeding success early in 1977, distinguishing himself as the first private American breeder to do so. A male from the 1976 SCZ clutch, acquired by Walsh, went on to sire much of the early founder stock and his bloodline is still represented in collections and breeding groups today. He is also one of the longest-lived chondros in captivity, having survived over 20 years in the collection of the Smithsonian's National Zoological Park (NZP).

Most of the original imported females did not survive to reproduce and those that did seldom lived long after their first clutch. In 1979, Indonesia imposed restrictions on exporting anything other than captive bred tree pythons, and at that point the flow of *legally* imported chondros into the U.S. ceased. By the early to mid eighties, however, enough captive bred chondros had been produced from the early imports to establish colonies. Al Zulich, of Harford Reptile Breeding Center in Maryland, was one of

The author produced this female (GM-00-08) in 2000; she is a fourth-generation offspring from both the 1976 SCZ breeding and the 1977 Walsh breeding.

those to establish a breeding colony. His blue female (then a very rare color morph) produced one of the early captive bloodlines still represented in collections today, and one that is involved in some of the current high-end projects.

Soon after his initial success, Walsh teamed up with another python breeder, Eugene Bessette of Ophiological Services (OS) in Gainesville, Florida. Dr. L.H.S. Van Mierop, who had been working with Bessette to study thermoregulation in brooding pythons, brought the two of them together. Van Mierop is credited with the early studies involving thermoregulation of brooding female chondros and with working out the temperature regimen used by the females to incubate their eggs. Walsh and Bessette formed a working relationship to study and reproduce chondros, attempting to solve the difficulties of captive breeding which was still very much a hit or miss endeavor. Their goals also included marketing captive bred pythons to other collectors and breeders. That collaboration has lasted over two decades and has made Walsh and Bessette "household names" to those interested in keeping and breeding GTPs. Together, they pioneered many of the procedures and techniques still used today and they have worked hard to promote the buying of captive bred chondros only. The OS slogan "Buy the best, forget the rest" reflects the commitment to quality that both of these men brought to the captive breeding and selling of GTPs. It is a testament to their success that these words now apply to the work of many breeders, who are carrying on that same commitment to quality. We owe them a debt of respect and gratitude for laying that foundation.

More Breeders and More Chondros

In the 1980s and 1990s, interest in captive bred reptiles of all kinds grew rapidly. In 1988, veteran keeper and breeder Don Hamper of Ohio started a monthly herp swap meet, and soon swap meets, shows, and expos became very popular. This in turn fueled the interest in reptiles and by the early 90s, captive bred snakes of many different kinds and of many different captive-developed color morphs were available to everyone. None of this enthusiasm and momentum was lost to chondro aficionados, and with the strides in breeding success made by the early pioneers, others began to enjoy a modest success rate with the species as well.

As more chondros were produced, and more information was shared, the captive breeding pool in the U.S. became firmly established. The chondro bug bit me hard in the early 90s, at which time I was maintaining a large colubrid collection, as well as running CageMaster, the reptile cage manufacturing and distributing company I founded in 1991. I began to assemble a sizable collection of captive bred chondros and by the late 90s I was consistently producing clutches of GTPs. I phased out keeping and breeding anything else, to focus exclusively on working with that species. Other successful chondro breeders during this time included, but certainly wasn't limited to: Al Zulich, already mentioned; Tim Turmezie, founder of the "Lemon Tree" bloodline; Dave and Tracy Barker; Tony Nicoli; Gary Sipperly of San Diego Reptile Breeders; Winslow Murdoch; Craig Trumbower; and Rob Worrell. Worrell is credited with observing and documenting that ovulation takes place approximately forty days prior to egg deposition in chondros, and for advances in the understanding of artificial incubation.

Imported chondros, legal and otherwise, continued to flow into the U.S., and even more so as the swap meet phenomenon created a huge new demand for reptiles. Much of the buying public, uninformed about the merits of buying captive bred and the pitfalls of buying imports, looked at price alone and usually paid for the mistake with disappointment and the feeling that chondros were too difficult to successfully keep. A few breeders, myself included, have fought long and hard (and sometimes loudly) to educate buyers about obtaining captive bred animals only, and how to tell the difference. To be sure, this has been (and still is) an uphill battle, but much progress has been made despite the shifting methods of some importers to disguise what they are selling. Much more will be said about this later.

Chondros and the Internet

I think it is safe to say that the invention of the World Wide Web, and its accessibility to the masses, will go down in history as one of the biggest influences on life in the late twentieth century. The Internet has made a way for instant, global communication to become a part of daily life for millions, and it is still growing and evolving. "Dot Com" companies have made (and lost) millions, and few and far between are the business interests that do not have a web presence, or have not tapped into the incredible potential of this vehicle for networking and advertising.

The rapidly expanding reptile industry, still gaining momentum from the influx of new hobbyists and more and better captive bred animals, gradually began to adopt the new Internet as a way of inexpensively and effectively marketing animals. The web also provided a great new way of networking between those with specialized interests, and of hosting discussion groups. Discussion forums sprang up, and some forums devoted to popular species became very active. One of these discussion groups, dedicated initially to locality specific Gray Banded Kingsnakes, grew into Kingsnake.com (KS), largely regarded as one of the biggest and most active reptile web sites on the Internet. In 1998, I launched my own web site, "Fine Green Tree Pythons, by Greg Maxwell", which has become the most popular GTP dedicated site on the Internet.

KS played host to an ever-increasing group of forums, each dedicated to a particular topic or species. Of course, all this Internet activity caught the attention of GTP enthusiasts, and chondros became such a popular topic on the "Python Forum" that eventually they were given a dedicated forum of their own. I was involved on the KS Python Forum as well as the KS Green Tree Python Forum from its inception and served as one of the "resident experts", answering questions and providing help and information to users of many levels of experience. While I am not comfortable being designated an "expert" about anything, I did have many years of experience and results to bring to the table, and for a while I was one of a very small group of people that were qualified, able, and willing to handle the daily task of answering chondro husbandry and breeding questions, many of them the same ones over and over. However, I realized that each new person was excited about learning all he or she could about these fascinating animals and so I took on the task with enthusiasm.

As the number of forums grew, and the popularity of the most active forums increased, moderation became a problem. Self-styled "experts" with little or no experience or results jockeyed for attention and juveniles with no apparent education about grammar or punctuation used the boards for daily playgrounds. As many people know, the biggest problem with the Internet is that anybody can say literally anything. If knowledgeable and experienced people don't correct errors and keep things on track, then bad information spreads rapidly and confusion abounds. If these people do stand up and speak, those corrected can become openly hostile, and if forum moderators don't control this then good forums can be quickly ruined. At one point, the strife became so bad that KS shut down all of its forums for a brief period. More than one forum was left closed, but those that remained open continued to allow a "free for all" atmosphere. Those who were intent on having intelligent discussions grew more and more frustrated with the situation, and most serious users got fed up and left. Unfortunately, human nature being what it is, this situation is doomed to be repeated anywhere mature and qualified moderators are not actively involved with Internet forums.

The Chondroweb Forums has become a daily meeting place to make friends and talk chondros for hundreds of 'chondroheads' from all over the world.

In the midst of all this, Thomas Phillips (Webmaster of ChondroWeb.com, a site dedicated to gathering and organizing information, web sites, breeders, and other data for use by the chondro community) and I decided to build our own forum. We simply had a vision for what we believed a forum should be, and for what the majority of the community needed and wanted. Launched in September 2000, the Chondroweb ChondroForum rapidly grew and it was soon obvious that Tomm and I were correct: there was a need and a desire for a clean, accurate, and well-run forum where enthusiasts of every level of skill and experience could share and learn, all within a properly moderated environment. In less than two years, the Chondroweb Forums (a Photography Forum, a Breeder Forum, and an Interactive Classifieds Forum were added) have become a model for Internet reptile forums. With hits exceeding 200,000 in 2001 and surpassing the one million mark early in 2003, the ChondroForums have become the most active Internet forums dedicated to a single reptile species, according to data and statistics at the time of writing. Noted for its professional and civil tone, and a dedication to quality, accuracy, and great photography, the Forum is the information site of choice for many of the best keepers and breeders around.

With the ability for GTP breeders and keepers to share information so easily, successful chondro keeping and breeding has continued to increase measurably. Strides have been especially noticeable in the area of artificial incubation, which was considered very difficult, and nearly impossible to get right on the first attempt, not all that long ago. This is directly due to the availability of good information, and access to those who have the experience to help, via the web. New breeders now have a way to introduce themselves to the market, and established breeders are no longer limited to bringing delicate animals to swap meets and expos to sell them. Although not without its frustrating issues, the World Wide Web has opened up a whole new arena of enjoyment, information, and success, to chondro lovers worldwide.

The Future of Chondros in Captivity

With the success of more and more hobbyists reproducing the species in captivity, it is obvious that the supply of healthy, captive bred stock is increasing. Some see this as a threat to the commercial value of chondros, but I disagree. While it is true that the number of enthusiasts is at an all-time high, there is still a huge, untapped market to be reached. My position has always been that as more individuals experience success in both keeping and breeding their animals, *the more they will pass on that passion to others. Passion is what has built the market to the present level, and passion is what will continue to build and expand it.* I know of no other reptile that evokes the same kind of dedication, passion, even obsession, as chondros do. The saying "You can't have just one" is literally true! This is why I have always been willing to share everything I know, and don't have "trade secrets" that I hold back. If I

GM-01-30 Truly, the sky is the limit to what is possible with the variations of colors and patterns being developed today.

help you succeed, you will hopefully in turn help someone else, and so on. Perhaps if chondros bred and fed like Cornsnakes, market saturation would become a problem. The truth is, the importation of wild collected and "farm raised" animals in bulk numbers is far more deleterious to the value of the chondro market than domestic breeders who are succeeding too well. Besides, as long as chondros are being bred, there will be neonates to get started, and that is one important ingredient that will always limit the amount of animals that make it to market, at least by honest sellers. Many of the more difficult aspects of chondro breeding have been smoothed by the spread of good information, but the feeding of neonates can test the skills and patience of many beyond what they are willing to deal with. Chondros are not Cornsnakes, and they never will be.

While the increase in the supply of captive bred stock will inevitably lead to some decrease in the average price for entry-level animals, I feel strongly that there will never be a huge chondro price crash like other species have experienced. Such a crash has been predicted to me for years, but I've yet to see it take place. Instead, if anything the opposite is true. Chondros are truly unique among the species of reptiles commonly being bred in captivity, in that they have shown themselves to be remarkably resilient in the face of general market decline and falling prices over the last several years. Further, their extreme variability of coloration and pattern has virtually eliminated the stagnation that other types of reptiles have experienced. With many reptiles, "you've seen one, you've seen them all", but chondros are the snowflakes of the snake world… each one has it's own unique beauty. Now, with the high-end "designer" morph projects being developed, the future of chondro breeding is wide open, and ripe with possibilities. With the recent hatch of the world's first living albino, even more fantastic breeding projects are on the horizon. In an early 2002 ChondroForum poll about albinos, 74% of those responding stated that they believed that the first albino would be worth over $50,000, and 33% said over $100,000. Over half said that they believed an albino would be produced in captivity in the next five to ten years. What a great surprise that the event occurred later that same year! Truly, this is a species whose morphological potential is limitless.

To most, chondros are a hobby and always will be. Others, like myself, are commercial breeders that make a living from breeding reptiles, including chondros. While some look on what I do as driven by greed, I disagree. As long as the animals are treated with the humane respect they deserve, and customers are given honesty and quality, then there is no reason to criticize someone for making a living doing something they love. The high prices commanded by the top animals are the natural result of the market forces of supply and demand. The truth is, there are always a few people that "demand" that breeders "supply" them with their best animals for minimal prices, and are offended because they can't afford them. However, that is not the way the free enterprise system works.

There is a healthy, self-sustaining and genetically diverse population of chondros in the U.S. today. There is also a growing number of enthusiasts, and more and better information available to those who want to take on the challenges of keeping and breeding these beautiful and mysterious rain forest serpents. Due to the communication possibilities of the Internet, European, as well as breeders from other continents, are having more dialog with American breeders than ever before. The future of the GTP in captivity is bright indeed.

Chapter 3. Geographic Races and Locality Typing

"The great majority of mankind are satisfied with appearances, as though they were realities, and are often even more influenced by the things that seem than by those that are."

Machiavelli

I'm sure that not a few of my readers turned to this chapter first to see what I would write concerning this controversial topic! I hope that anyone who feels, as I do, that chondro locality issues are important will take the time to carefully and thoughtfully read the information presented here. Consider the facts as well as my opinions, which I will make every effort to separate. I also ask that the reader consider *all* the information presented here and not react negatively to a single statement or position taken out of context.

In recent years, the locality debates have spun out of control, and as with most controversial issues, the truth seldom lies with extreme views from either side. The position that every chondro is identifiable as to locality is ridiculous; so is the attitude that all locality claims are false. I have done my fair share of debating with those who tend to make unsubstantiated locality claims, and I have argued long and hard for the chondro community to insist on the facts and documentation when considering such claims. This has gotten me the reputation for being "closed-minded", and one who categorically rejects all chondro locality claims. This is simply not true. I would state for the record that questioning data and doing some critical thinking does not make one "closed-minded". If that were true, then every legitimate scientist is "closed-minded". Too many people today define being "open-minded" as agreeing with them!

The truth is, an awful lot of what washes for locality specifications are simply claims made by importers, dealers, and brokers, to give credibility to otherwise inferior animals. By inferior, I mean animals that are not up to par with the robust, healthy captive bred stock offered by dedicated domestic breeders, or those not able to be categorized as belonging to any one of the specialty color morphs being bred. By labeling an individual chondro with some locality name, the seller hopes to give an impression of added value. This mindset has so permeated the mass marketing of

Q: Can you identify the locality of this chondro? A: No, because it is a mixed-ancestry CB animal with no collection data for the WC parents. It was produced in 1999 by Janet Hickner... Isn't it beautiful?

GTPs by animal dealers that recently an acquaintance of mine found it impossible to sell some animals of his on a large online classified page because he refused to make up a locality for his stock. One respondent after another told him if the animal wasn't "locality" they didn't want it. Besides questioning why knowing the supposed geographic origin of an animal is so magical, I would ask these buyers how they think that some second or third party involved in the sale could possibly have accurate information about the capture location of a specimen.

Some Definitions

I think that right up front, before getting into the nuts and bolts of the discussion, it is important to establish some definitions of the terms used. A lot of potential confusion can be avoided if those discussing locality and race issues understand and properly apply the correct definitions to the words that are sometimes thrown around a bit too loosely. Let's look specifically at two of these terms: Locality and Race.

Locality

Locality, in the context of describing a biological specimen, refers to the exact location where the particular specimen was collected. Webster's dictionary defines locality as "a particular place". The whole concept of locality-specific reptiles was popularized by a group of Gray Banded Kingsnake (*Lampropeltis alterna*) collectors. These *alterna* fans placed a premium on specimens that had exact collecting data and believed that individual locality populations had unique characteristics that made them different from other populations. This sparked the popularity of a whole new concept in reptile collecting and marketing... the "locality" specimen. Leaving aside questions about the validity of the belief that such locality *alterna* are more valuable or desirable than other specimens of that group, the important point to remember is that these hobbyists have the ability to collect their own snakes, and to carefully document the exact collection point of each animal. The more accurate the collecting data obtained, and the higher the credibility of the collector, the greater the value of the specimen, according to these locality fans. It is important to note that it is the documented geographic origin of the specimen that identifies it as a locality-specific animal, **not its outward appearance**. Most dedicated locality *alterna* collectors are very skeptical of undocumented locality claims, or claims based on mere morphological traits.

Race

Webster defines race as "a family, tribe, people, or nation of the same stock". When discussing GTP race distinctions, it is important to understand that these are based on external, identifiable traits.

Biologist Dr. Guido Westhoff made this clarification between race and locality recently in a reply to a question about locality and race differences on the ChondroForum: "There sure is a difference! A "locality" just describes that an animal comes from a certain geographic location... a locality therefore doesn't describe any specific character or feature of that animal... just the geographic origin is the point regardless of morphological relevance."

Dr. Westhoff continues: "A "race" is always determined by certain characteristics (look at dogs: German shepherds, poodles and so on). A race is not taxonomically of any value because a race just describes a bundle of features and characters that can be found in man-made or natural populations. A natural race may have the status of a subspecies but that's not always the case."

If the difference between these two terms would be understood and applied, what a lot of misunderstanding and confusion could be avoided when statements regarding locality are made!

Just the facts, Ma'am

Applying these two definitions to the present topic, it is quite easy to see that there are very few true locality-specific chondros around. For one thing, it is illegal for Indonesian dealers to export any wild caught chondro. While this minor technicality hasn't stopped many of them, they certainly aren't sending out valid collection data along with the animals. Second, the remoteness of the region and the current political instability make it quite unattractive for foreign would-be collectors. Third, it is well known that the native collectors gather specimens from wherever they find them, and bring them to holding facilities pending exportation. Often these holding pens are cold, dirty, and crowded. Many of the most popular "locality" names are simply the names of Indonesian cities near collection sites, and that have airports readily accessible for shipping the animals out. This would be akin to naming some randomly collected Gray Banded Kingsnakes "El Paso" locality because that was the nearest town with an airport. So to be perfectly fair and honest, how many wild collected GTPs can be accurately represented as "locality"? And by definition, captive produced animals, unless from documented locality-specific founder stock, *cannot* be locality animals because locality means "collected from a specific geographic location".

So, are there any bonafide locality-specific chondros? Absolutely! I'm personally aware of several such projects. In each case, the breeders are working with animals that have a documented, unbroken trail back to the collecting locations of the founder stock. In one case, the breeder even has a map showing the jeep trail leading to the collection point. In another, a missionary known to the breeder actually hand-carried a chondro from Biak and brought it back to the States. Such animals, and the accompanying documentation, are very hard to come by. High standards for sorting the facts, and sound ethics, are required for credibility. There are good reasons to resist taking just anybody's word for things, especially when making money off of the information is an issue. To the point, some animal dealers will say anything they think (or know) a buyer wants to hear, in order to make sales.

In addition to private collectors who are fortunate enough to have made the contacts to acquire legitimate locality-specific founder stock, a couple of Indonesian reptile dealers claim to have set up *in situ* breeding programs using locality-specific founder stock. Bushmaster Reptiles, D&J Reptiles, and Arboreals Plus are all importing and brokering chondros from overseas sources that are reported to be both captive bred and locality-specific. It is not my purpose here to comment on the credibility of any particular company or source. I have corresponded with Freek Nuyt, the European breeder supplying Arboreals Plus with CB neonates, and found him to be knowledgeable and helpful. Some of his observations are included later in this chapter. Herpafauna Indonesia, supplier to D&J, has reportedly implanted microchips in their breeders. While this would be very useful for tracking the movements of specific captive animals within the large outdoor enclosures used by HI, and also of great value in identifying stolen animals, such microchips would be of no value as locality identifiers unless they were implanted and logged at the location of capture. As we are about to discover however, it is the author's opinion that the majority of the captive "locality" breeding being done, both in the U.S. and abroad, would more accurately be described as "race specific"- that is, selective breeding based on external morphological traits, often with no accurate collection data for the founder stock.

Geographic Races of the Green Tree Python

We have seen that true locality-specific animals of any species earn that designation by having been collected from a documented geographic location, regardless of appearance. A race, on the other hand, refers to a group of specimens that share distinct morphological traits. Let us turn our attention to the race issue as it relates to GTPs.

There are at least four distinct naturally occurring races of chondros recognized by most keepers and breeders. These are the Aru and Biak Island forms, the mainland Sorong race, and the Merauke or Cape York race. There has been some talk of recognizing one or more of these as a subspecies, but currently no such distinctions have been made. A brief description of each race is made below with emphasis on generally accepted color and pattern traits.

The Aru Island Race

The Aru Island group lies off the southwestern coast of West Papua, and is home to a race of chondros named after the main island. This race is noted for several characteristics, the most obvious of which is the sprinkling of white scales on a lime green body color. These white scales

This is a WC, undocumented Aru-type male that conforms to the phenotype description of this race.

are usually concentrated on the dorsal area and may appear singly or in small groups. They may also connect to form a partial dorsal stripe. It is quite probable that individuals of this race have made it to the southern coast of New Guinea as it is not uncommon to see white speckling on mainland animals. Some older specimens may have gray or silver scales mixed in with the white. Areas of blue pigment may or may not be mixed in with the white dorsal markings on some specimens, but a beautiful blue color on the lateral and belly area of the body is present on the best specimens, and can be quite stunning. The blue may also extend onto the lower and upper labials.

Typical short, blunt Aru tail.

Aru chondros often have a short, blunt tail; so much so that the impression is that the snake has lost the last few inches. The typical Aru chondro has a classic-shaped, medium-sized head with rounded lobes. They are medium-sized as adults, averaging about 60 inches in length, although the author has seen an adult female that exceeded 72 inches (see photo in Chapter 1). Individuals of this race are usually among the more tame and easy to handle of chondros, but there can be notable exceptions, especially when dealing with wild caught specimens. I consider keepers who suffer frequent bites to be lacking in handling know-how, and I take care to avoid being bitten, but one of the more severe chondro bites I have sustained came from a wild caught Aru female that I carelessly removed from a shipping container. The animal was reportedly a three-year captive at the time I received it, and I assumed that being of the Aru race, she would be safe to free-handle. I was quite wrong, and to this day she remains one of the most irritable and easily provoked adults in my collection, and the same thing can be said of her wild caught mate, seen in the photo on the opposite page.

The Biak Island Race

The second of the two island forms, the Biak race, certainly doesn't come in behind the others in terms of size, personality, and unique traits.

Typical CB Biak-type female.

Widely regarded as the largest of the species, Biaks can be impressive, with large heads, long dragon-like snouts, flared nostrils, long sharply pointed tails, and big bulky bodies. They also have a well-deserved reputation for being snappy and easily provoked.

Typical Biak head with large lobes and elongated snout. Photo courtesy of Damon Salceies.

A few keepers have challenged this last characterization as false. It is my belief that this opinion may have been formed while working with an occasional animal that does not conform to the norm; or perhaps while interacting with Biak out-crossed animals that aren't pure-blooded, and have benefited from the tempering effects of cross-breeding. Certainly most keepers who have been exposed to typical Biak animals are very much aware of the usual fiery temperament of these animals and smile wryly to themselves when they hear such protests.

Biak coloration tends to be more muted in adulthood than other types of chondros, but frequently includes some yellow. The green is often more pale than the other forms and is usually the dominant color, with blotches of yellow in varying degrees mixed in. The effect is unique and has been described by the wife of one of my customers as a "tie-dyed" look. Often some white is evident too, on single scales or more frequently as small "flowers" made of several scales. Specimens from the nearby Yapen Island are reported to commonly have these white flowers in profusion, often without the characteristic yellow. A very common Biak trait is a patch or bar of bright yellow on the face or nose.

Biak chondros typically undergo the ontogenic color change in a rather unique way, usually taking much longer than the other forms, and often exhibiting some beautiful and spectacular, if temporary, colors and patterns during the change. Those uninitiated to the long length of time and unusual colors associated with Biak yearling color changes can become quite excited, thinking they have acquired an extraordinary chondro, only to be disappointed as the animal adopts the more typical adult appearance as it matures. This can take as long as three to four years with some of these animals. Happily, when out-crossed with mainland specimens, Biak blood seems to be involved in a lot of the interesting results which selective captive breeding is producing. More about this will be said in the next chapter.

The Cape York (Merauke) Race

This race superficially resembles the Aru race in that it features lime green animals with white dorsal markings, and frequently with blue on the ventral and lateral areas. However, in the Cape York and Merauke form the white is reduced to a nearly solid vertebral stripe made up of mostly single scales.

WC locality-specific Merauke female. Photo courtesy of Damon Salceies.

The effect is clean and attractive, making these, the least common of the naturally occurring race morphs, highly desirable. At least this form is uncommon in collections; the strict export restrictions in place on all Australian wildlife have made it nearly impossible for any Cape York specimens to find their way into breeding programs. The Cape York Peninsula forms the northern-most extension of Australia and is believed to be the only part of that country where chondros are known to live. Merauke is a southern coastal city of West Papua (Irian Jaya) that lies just west of the PNG border and is close in proximity to the Cape York Peninsula.

There are a very few, true locality-specific Merauke specimens in the U.S. One group of these animals originated from an area south of the small village of Tanah Merah, which is north of Merauke. In 1996, Tracy Barker successfully bred two of these imports and the offspring are now in several private collections. One of those working with a group of these offspring, Damon Salceies, successfully produced a clutch in early 2002 from a sibling-to-sibling pairing. His locality breeding accomplishment

Trooper Walsh's Merauke male sired this outstanding male in the author's collection. The Walsh male is a sibling to those owned by Damon Salceies, parents of the first CB albino GTP.

was greatly upstaged when he announced in August of that year that two of the hatchlings were albino! Trooper Walsh produced a clutch in the spring of 2001 that was sired by a Merauke male from the same 1996 F1 group. These Merauke out-crossed offspring have developed into outstanding looking yearlings, but so far none seem to have the classic Merauke patterning. Very few of the young Merauke chondros in the Salceies F2 group are developing vertebral stripes (Salceies, pers. com.). For more about the Merauke albino project, see Chapter 4.

Mainland Forms (Sorong, Jayapura, and others)

Sorong is a coastal city on the Vogelkop peninsula at the western tip of West Papua (Irian Jaya), and has long lent its name to groups of chondros that have been collected and exported from the region. Far from being an actual "locality", Sorong is simply the name of the city where shipping out the animals has been facilitated by boat and air traffic. In reality, the New Guinea land mass is quite large and divided by a mountain range, and many variations exist in the appearance of the GTP specimens collected from different areas. Sorting out the differences and accurately describing the various groups is difficult to say the least, and there are widely varying opinions about the validity of doing so with any degree of accuracy. But perhaps Sorong is the most common name associated with a mainland race, and has come to be recognized as describing certain traits.

Most chondros with blue dorsal stripes and triangles are associated with the Sorong race. This is a CB female.

Sorong chondros are best recognized by a blue dorsal stripe, and blue triangular shaped dorsal markings. The quantity and intensity of the blue can be highly variable. Blue spots are frequently found on the body, as are blue head stripes. Some specimens have a few white scales and some are solid green. Other typical traits of the Sorong race include a smaller head with a shorter snout than the island forms, and a longer tail that is more pointed at the tip, than is typical of Aru animals. The tail is always pigmented with black or dark blue (Nuyt, pers. com.). Sorong chondros seem to be a bit smaller overall than other races. Temperament can run the gamut, but on average Sorong and other mainland forms tend to

Most mainland forms have smaller heads and shorter noses when compared with other races.

41

be fairly tractable.

Jayapura, another coastal city, located in north-central Irian Jaya near the Papua New Guinea border, also gets frequently mentioned as a chondro locality. Like Sorong, the name has been applied to chondros collected from the surrounding areas and exported. Papua New Guinea (PNG) is often used to indicate animals that are believed to originate from that country, which makes up the eastern half of the mainland area. Port Moresby is commonly named as the location of

Sorong specimens have dark pigmented, medium length tails.

Rico Walder produced this pretty female from PNG founder stock.

export and no other locality data is available for most PNG chondros, which are probably of mixed ancestry. There are several attractive and variable captive bred bloodlines that trace their roots to PNG origins. One notable line, developed by Rico Walder, has produced specimens including blue and high yellow. Lemon Tree chondros are also reportedly from PNG stock. Probably much of the early imported stock came from PNG, and Switak brought back his gravid female from this area in 1973 (see Chapter 2).

Confused? The fact is, mainland chondros are much more variable in color and patterns than are the more isolated island races. This makes sense, because the New Guinea land mass is quite large, and other than the mountain range that divides the country in half north and south, there aren't many limiting geophysical factors (other than possibly elevation) to divide GTP populations. Therefore, quite a bit of variation is seen in animals from different parts of the mainland. Color patterns of mainland chondros can range from solid green to those with yellow triangle markings, as well as the blue of typical Sorong specimens.

Micro-Localities

In recent years, some new and strange-sounding locality names have come into use, mostly in Internet classified ads. These so-called locality populations have been viewed with skepticism by much of the chondro community and have been largely assumed to be marketing ploys. There are several reasons for this: For one thing, some of these "new" locality claims have come from dealers who are not exactly the cream of the crop when it comes to reputation in the industry; further, attempts to obtain any kind of documentation about the legitimacy of these locations as unique chondro populations have been met with everything from indifference to outright hostility. In attempting to seek out the truth about these supposed localities, which include such names as Arfak, Wamena, Bokondini, Karubaga, Lereh, and others, I coined the label "micro-localities" to refer to them. As with several other locality and race names mentioned in this chapter, many of these micro-locality labels are based on the names of towns near to airports.

I have been collecting information for some time about the possibility of local populations of chondros with unique morphological characteristics that warrant specific designations. Good information has not been easy to obtain, and too many locality advocates quickly accept any locality claims as fact simply because the concept appeals to them. However, there is evidence that founder stock with collection data from some of

This attractive yellow juvenile was produced by European breeder Freek Nuyt and is represented as coming from Wamena locality founder stock.

these areas is being bred in captivity. As mentioned above, one of the problems with identifying local populations of mainland chondros is the fact that New Guinea has little in the way of geophysical conditions that would tend to limit and confine those populations, in the same manner that the island forms are. Obviously, there must be some limiting boundaries to a specific population in order for that population to develop distinct and separate characteristics. Otherwise, the intermingling of genes between mainland populations would preclude the evolution of distinct micro populations. Again I quote Dr. Westhoff:

"Usually phenotypes of species vary within their range. Depending on species this variation might be higher or lower. As we all know, the variation in chondros is high. Localities or subspecies of any species are usually defined by specific features and characteristics that occur only in a geographical isolated range. Three important things to define when considering such localities are:

1. The definition of characteristics and features (or combinations) that clearly do not occur in the rest of the range. To achieve this, one has to define the "types" inside the suspected locality range and outside this range.

2. The definition of the geographical range! A name of a town nearby is certainly not providing this most [important] argument to talk about a true "locality". Usually borders of the range of this [proposed] locality are drawn into a geographical map. This is absolutely necessary to make sure that the third point (below) is valid.

3. The borders of the range of the described locality must define the geographical isolation. In other words, the same species cannot live [as a] neighbor to that border. If that is the case and the first point is truly valid, we would have a case of no gene flow making our locality a new species (which is not the case, as crossbreeding localities proves). If there is another locality right next to our new locality type, we have to describe the size of the bastardizing zone (I won't go into detail about what a hybrid-zone and bastard-zone tells us about species and subspecies, they are a tool often used by taxonomists and evolution biologists). If the bastard zone is too large/broad, the first point (above) cannot be valid (especially in a "micro-locality").

Finally, I know none of these three points have been evaluated or considered with any accuracy for any mainland-chondro. However, they are most likely valid for the island forms. Most accurate documents on mainland localities are only as good as the definition of the locality itself! If there is no definition of character, described border or range, you just have a chondro that was caught nearby a town with a nice name.

I understand the arguments of purists concerning conservation of variation of chondros. However, when it comes to so called micro-localities, documented or not, I see the risk of conserving only a locality-tag produced by some local dealer or some hobbyists who just want to own some "special" chondro that others do not have."

I would add "the ability to claim to sell some special locality that others don't have" to Dr. Westhoff's last thought.

In balance, there are collectors and breeders who claim that local and regional populations of chondros with recognizable, if subtle, traits do exist. Efforts are being made by some to establish breeding groups that reproduce these traits. Several non-American breeders have on-site collecting experience and claim documentation of the geographic origin of their founder animals. According to information and descriptions about some of the mainland forms I've been able to obtain, the names Wamena, Bokondini, and Karubaga all refer to the same specimens from the same area, and there isn't a valid reason to consider them as separate localities. However, one breeder does feel that there are enough differences in color, pattern, build, and possibly scalation between Wamena animals and those from Lereh to warrant distinction. These two mountain locations are not connected and are sufficiently far enough apart to produce GTPs with their own unique traits (Nuyt, pers. com.). It is possible that mountain elevation could be a defining boundary for some of these populations, which have been labeled as "highland" localities by those working with them. Mr. Nuyt has indicated to me that distinctions can be made between these two highland forms and low elevation Sorong specimens, based on morphological differences than include tail shape and color, and the shape and hue of the blue dorsal markings.

Some specimens reported to have been collected from upper elevation sites tend to go through a heavily speckled stage during the ontogenic color change. Some animals keep the dark pigment in varying degrees, but many lose it altogether as they mature. One theory is that the darker coloration aids the animals in gathering heat from the sun's rays, from which reptiles living in the cooler temperatures found at the higher elevations would benefit. This would not explain why many of the animals lose the dark pigment; certainly chondros don't need warmth only while yearlings. Perhaps the dark pigment is a coincidence and is a random trait in some animals collected from that part of the country. This same phenomenon can be seen in captive bred bloodlines that have no known relationship with any highland stock. Nonetheless, breeders working with designated highland localities are enthusiastic about them, and perhaps in the future some of the questions about these and other micro-localities can be answered.

Although indigenous collectors and exporters with enough experience may come to recognize that specimens from certain areas tend to show certain traits, it is still essential to have valid documentation for true locality specimens. Chondros are far too variable in color and pattern to make firm conclusions about origin without verifiable collecting data. In reality, too much of what passes for locality identification is simply speculation and wishful thinking, and attempting to guess the origins of undocumented CB specimens is nearly useless. Locality animals are identified by specific data, not guesses. Recognized race names can serve to identify general morphological traits and provide some common ground for collectors and breeders to use when referring to various groups. But in truth, without collecting documentation, these specimens should not be represented as locality specific. To do so is not only inaccurate, but can be downright dishonest, and it does a huge disservice to those who have put in the time and work to properly validate the locality specimens they are working with.

Race and locality "Type" Chondros

In this chapter I have described several recognized and somewhat distinct races of GTPs. As has also been made apparent, it is almost always up to the persons working with the animals to judge and distinguish between these races based on generally accepted phenotypes. In some cases, this can be done with reasonable confidence; a classic Biak looks nothing like a classic Aru. Too much of the time, chondros fail to look "classic" and can bewilder the would-be classifier with a wide range of variability, even within a particular race group. Add to this the fact that mainland animals are far less likely to adhere to rigid descriptions and the possibility exists for all kinds of confusion, guesswork, and even misrepresentation. Several years ago, I began to promote the use of the word "type" to designate specimens that conformed to established race descriptions, but at the same time had no real documentation. Hence, "Aru-type" was used to indicate an animal that exhibited enough of the typical Aru traits to be labeled an Aru, but that in all honesty could not be proven to have come from pure Aru founder stock. This designation has really caught on and has provided a way (for those who wish to do so) to have a valid and honest way to describe and discuss animals so that everybody involved knows exactly what is being claimed and presented for consideration.

Locality-specific and Racially-pure Breeding

Many factors motivate people to breed chondros in captivity. The fascination of seeing new life come to be through our efforts, the overcoming of difficulties and conquering of the challenges, and the desire to profit financially from doing something worthwhile can all play a role. Equally diverse are the tastes and values that determine the direction we take when deciding what animals to work with and what projects to give priority to. There have always been those who favor working with naturally occurring color morphs rather than those produced by selective breeding, and which can be highly unusual and may bear no resemblance to wild specimens. I feel that there is plenty of room for both pursuits. In fact, I consider myself a fan of each. Where I draw the line is at the notion that one kind of breeding program is somehow morally superior to another.

In reality, unless a breeder has detailed, specific documentation about his founder animals (such as was noted with the Merauke project), he or she is simply endeavoring to reinforce desirable traits by selective breeding and is engaged in the same process as those breeding designer morphs. Both types of breeding reflect human tastes and opinions; neither is morally superior to the other. Even the locality-specific breeder with his or her group of carefully documented animals, be they *alterna* or *viridis*, is making choices and manipulations that almost certainly would not be duplicated exactly in nature, and this only becomes more true with each successive generation that is produced.

I am not an advocate of the extremist view that anything man touches or influences is somehow perverted or tainted. I do agree with those who feel it would be a sad loss if specific natural populations were to be wiped out, for any reason, natural or otherwise. I think we as humans have an obligation to manage wildlife and wild habitats in a responsible manner, conserving and preserving wild populations in a balanced approach that takes all factors into consideration. I have no quarrel with those who seek to maintain breeding colonies that reflect, as closely as possible, the natural appearance of wild chondro populations. I reject the assertion that to do otherwise is unethical, immoral, or irresponsible. Perhaps the two most important things an individual can do regarding wild GTP preservation is to *avoid buying wild caught imports*, a practice which supports an industry that is not promoting the best interests of either the customers or the wild populations; and to support and promote those who are working to stop or reverse habitat destruction.

It bears repeating: a breeder working with Sorong-type animals (as one example) that have been visually selected for morphological traits is not doing "locality breeding". Rather, he or she is engaged in selectively breeding for chosen characteristics, the same as another breeder might work to produce high yellow animals. Both are doing what they enjoy and as long as both of them are honest with the public and treat the animals with humane respect, then both are to be applauded.

In closing the discussion about this controversial subject, allow me to recap the important points I've made in this chapter:

> "Locality" means a specific geographic collection location and the chondros collected there, *regardless of appearance*.

"Race" refers to a group of chondros that share unique, distinguishable traits.

Race and Locality are not the same thing; most chondros conform more to racial descriptions than to the narrow definition of a locality animal.

Island forms constitute the most easily recognized race groups because an island represents a physical barrier that tends to concentrate the morphologic traits of the inhabitants and keeps other groups from influencing them under normal circumstances.

For a chondro to be accurately labeled with a locality name, *documentation for the collection site must be available.* This is not merely an opinion; it goes to the very definition of the word.

Many chondros can be grouped according to race, and the designation of "type" indicates the animal has sufficient traits to be categorized within one of the recognized race groups, but does not have documentation of its wild origins.

The more generations of captive breeding that take place within a bloodline, the less accurate any locality-specific designations will be, and many captive bred animals can not be accurately identified as to locality or race. Breeders in several countries are working to preserve the integrity of the appearances of naturally occurring geographic races, including those from smaller, higher elevation collecting sites.

It is sincerely hoped that the information and opinions offered here would go a long way toward eliminating the confusion and division that has been all too common in the chondro community regarding the locality debate. I don't think I have asked for anything unreasonable in what I have written. Those interested in the truth, and committed to searching out the facts, should not have a problem with being asked to back up their claims and beliefs with evidence, good science, and solid logic. There will always be a few who have an agenda to accomplish and who react in a negative manner when confronted with the issues and questions raised here. Nothing constructive can be accomplished by arguing with those who aren't interested in facts and who have their minds made up. To the rest, I say let us continue to work together, sharing data and learning new things that will enhance our enjoyment and appreciation of these beautiful and mysterious pythons. As long as we all pursue our goals with an open mind, focused on facts and sound data, we can't help but arrive at the same destination! We may not always agree or interpret data in the same way, but we can respect each other's positions so long as they are reached and expressed with intelligence and integrity.

Chapter 4. Designer Color and Pattern Morphs, and GTP Genetics

"There is no excellent beauty that hath not some strangeness in the proportion."

Francis Bacon

"Grace" (GM-99-04) This beautiful female, produced by the author in 1999, is half Lemon Tree.

I have to say that I'm not completely comfortable with the term "designer". This always conjures up an image in my mind of someone with a recipe book of bizarre colors and patterns, which they mix and match until they get just the right effect before somehow implanting these colors onto their animals. The word also seems to imply that people have the ability to control the results of their breeding. The fact is, there isn't a single one of us that has the power to create the spark of life in another creature, let alone exercise control over the complicated genetics involved in the beautiful and highly variable colors found on GTPs. Nonetheless, it is true that many of these specialty morphs are the result of human efforts and manipulations, and animals are produced from these that would not occur in natural populations, at least under normal circumstances. Certainly any wild individuals with such stand-out colors would not be a good survival bet.

I also am hesitant to use the phrase "high-end" to describe certain color morphs. From the perspective of demand and value, it is true that some of the specialty lines are quite "high up" on the measure of worth and desirability, but I fear that to describe such specimens as high-end gives the impression that other animals may be "low-end". Again, from a purely commercial consideration this may be accurate, but it sounds arrogant and elitist. While certainly there are lesser and greater chondros within the context of health and vitality, any captive bred, healthy chondro is of great worth as a beautiful animal and as someone's prized possession. Perhaps "high-end" is better used to describe outstanding specimens of any color or pattern, natural or humanly influenced, rather than applied just to extreme captive produced morphs. Since both "designer" and "high end" have come into relatively common use, and everyone knows what they mean, I will use them in this book and in this chapter. Maybe sometime soon we will come up with a good way to refer to these selectively bred, captive-produced color morphs that doesn't have the possible negative connotations the current terms do. One thing is sure; the morphs themselves are wildly popular! The extreme variability of colors and patterns that chondros are able to exhibit has resulted in the development of captive bloodlines with the goal of fixing these traits, more or less, into reliable and trustworthy genetic characteristics. A lot of progress has been made in the last few years and several distinct color morphs have been established as inheritable traits and have become a part of many collectors' wish lists. Even naturally occurring color and pattern traits can be improved by pairing above average specimens of race-specific specimens; high white Arus are but one example, and would also be considered by many to be "high-end".

Before getting into a detailed description of the existing morphs, and the future of designer morph breeding, it would be wise to discuss the matter of GTP genetics. A realistic understanding of this topic is vital to begin unraveling the mysteries of selective breeding and morph development. We will also discuss the ontogenic color change and the different color phases of neonate chondros.

Chondro Genetics

Usually the first thing someone will ask after seeing an unusually colored or marked tree python is, "Do you think that is genetic?" What they actually want to know is if the trait is inheritable, and if so, how reliably it will be passed on. Every trait of any living organism is "genetic", but not all traits may be heritable, and not all heritable traits are the result of simple dominant or recessive genes. Confused? You are not alone! And while I'm the first to admit that I am not a geneticist, I do have some basic understanding about these things. Furthermore, I can make some solid observations about how genetics work when considering chondro colors and other morphological traits, having made this an area of personal research and study for a number of years. In fact, my interest and observations about the genetics of reptile breeding predates my work with chondros. My purpose here is not to attempt to make genetics experts out of us, but rather to enable the reader to grasp the important and foundational truths necessary for sorting out the facts from fiction regarding what makes these highly variable animals look like they do. Lets wade in and see if we can make some sense of this confusing and mysterious aspect of GTP biology.

It would be good to begin with some basic definitions of "terms of heredity". Barry C. Nielsen supplied these definitions on his excellent web site, "The Advanced Genetics Wizard", and they are used by permission. Please see Appendix B for the web address.

Allele - *either of the two paired genes affecting an inherited trait (one from the father, one from the mother)*

Co-dominant - *an allele that causes the homozygous form to look different than wild type and the heterozygous form to have traits of both. (All three look different from each other)*

Dominant - *an allele that causes the homozygous form and the heterozygous form to look the same as each other, but different than wild type*

Recessive - *an allele that affects an animal's appearance if it's present in the homozygous state only; an animal that's heterozygous for a mutant, recessive gene looks wild type, but that gene can be passed on to offspring*

Heterozygous - *having two different alleles for a genetic trait*

Homozygous - *having identical alleles for a genetic trait*

Wild Type - *the way an animal looks with the greatest frequency in a wild population ("normal")*

Now, let us attempt to apply these definitions to chondros in a way we can understand and that relate to practical, real-life examples. Obviously, a "Wild Type" chondro would be an example of one of the basic race descriptions given in the previous chapter. For the sake of the discussion, let's use a wild caught specimen of the Biak race as an example. This animal has all the basic outward appearances typical of the race description for Biaks. Now, say we cross this animal with a "Wild Type" mainland female that shows typical Sorong characteristics. Let's further extend this hypothetical but realistic example to show that of 16 offspring produced, several of them have more than a usual amount of yellow when they mature, while the rest look more or less like the female that produced them. One may even be said to have "high yellow" coloration.

Normally, we would then make the assumption that the high yellow trait was a recessive gene passed down from the parents. In other words, both parents would have to be heterozygous for high yellow, but would appear normal (wild type) themselves. Neither parent can be dominant or homozygous, because then they would exhibit high yellow coloration too. But there are several problems when applying this understanding to our example. First, what are the odds that two random and completely unrelated adults would be carrying compatible alleles for the yellow trait? Second, there should be fairly predictable results that can be calculated for the offspring of recessive parents, using the familiar Punnet Square. But when the offspring of adult chondros are tracked, they seldom if ever develop along the expected mathematical ratios that traditional predictors would indicate. Third, GTP traits often visually express themselves inconsistently even within the same clutch, rather than as definable and clearly distinguishable traits. This is why we have "high yellow" adults rather than just simply "yellow". Six different offspring from the same parents can have six different amounts of yellow on them and it is up to the eye of the beholder to determine what is "high" and what isn't. Compare this to an actual dominant or recessive trait, such as albinism, which is either expressed in an individual animal or it isn't. There are no "high albinos".

What we do tend to observe in chondros are two phenomenon: An unusual tendency for spontaneous color mutations to randomly surface;

and the tendency for various traits to develop in gradients, and over time with selective breeding, rather than being expressed in predictable and reliable percentages. It is important to repeat that this does *not* mean these traits aren't genetic or inheritable. But it *does* mean that the results of breeding specific pairs for specific traits cannot be predicted with any degree of certainty unless there is some history of documented results.

We can observe this same principle when breeding dogs. Many of the desired characteristics of show, field trial, or hunting dogs are developed over time, and by mating parents that have these traits themselves. Even so, any given litter of pups is likely to have a range of results, with one pup being judged the pick of the litter and the others ranked in descending order. Consider a characteristic such as size; in a litter of puppies there will be random results. These results can be strengthened over time, and breeding larger examples of the same breed of dog will tend to develop puppies that will grow to be large adults, with results expressed in a gradient. With chondros, color and pattern seem to follow this same trend, rather than being expressed as a dominant or recessive gene. With Labrador Retrievers, color is a trait that is expressed as a dominant or recessive gene, and fairly predictable results can be obtained when crossing adults of known genetic traits. However, adult size variations and other canine characteristics such as hip problems are seen randomly and are much less predictable, although they are still very much influenced by the family tree. With chondros, the color traits have not demonstrated themselves to be simple dominant or recessive genes, although they are definitely influenced by ancestry as well.

What this means in plain language is that you can't be sure of getting high yellow offspring from breeding one or more high yellow parents.

The same thing is true for high blue animals or several other popular color or pattern morphs. Fortunately, most of these traits do tend to strengthen with selective breeding, and much more so in some bloodlines than in others. For example, the Lemon Tree bloodline, which refers specifically to animals from the Tim Turmezie high yellow bloodline, has demonstrated itself to be very potent. One of my Lemon Tree females has produced high yellow offspring with two different males, neither of which had any known relation to the LT line. Other high yellow bloodlines have produced some random and exquisitely colored specimens, but with less consistency than the LT line. Other designer morph bloodlines have shown varying degrees of success producing offspring with the same or better characteristics than the parents.

What conclusions can be drawn from all of this, especially in light of some of the prices charged for designer morph offspring? Certainly the most important is to include the reproductive history of the parents in the decision-making process when choosing offspring. When adults that show high-end characteristics reproduce, the offspring are certainly worth more than offspring from more normal-looking adults, because the odds of getting an unusual or outstanding specimen from such a clutch are definitely higher. But collectors need to understand that buying such offspring is in fact a decision involving some degree of risk. The more detailed the reproductive history of one or both parents, the better your knowledge about what you may be getting. Conversely, parents with no available history represent the highest risk. Also, the fact that one animal has produced high-end offspring in the past is no certain indicator that it will do so again when being bred to a different mate.

Offspring often strongly reflect the traits of one parent over the other; breeder chondros that have demonstrated the ability to produce high-end offspring with multiple mates are valuable indeed. Pairs that repeatedly produce consistent results when bred to each other represent the most secure choice when buying offspring in the hope of obtaining a specific result. Since specific designer morph breeding is still relatively new, it can be stated that much of the designer breeding being done currently is still in the experimental and developmental stages.

Color Phases of Neonate Chondros

Baby chondros come in two basic phases… golden yellow and maroon. I refer to these as color phases because a phase is temporary, and certainly the baby colors are not permanent. There is wide and sometimes

A reduced-pattern yellow neonate produced by the author from a high yellow bloodline.

extreme variation within these two phases however!

Some examples of this variation can be seen in the photos of the neonates throughout this book. The yellow babies usually have a pattern of red or brown speckling, bars, spots, or geometric shapes on a beautiful bright yellow body. They may also have white markings, usually in the center of the other shapes. Although the intensity and quantity of red or brown markings can vary, yellow babies normally show much less diversity than do dark babies. These dark offspring can be red, maroon, or brown, with much variation between individuals and from clutch to clutch. They have such rich, gorgeous colors that it is no wonder that they are the favorites of many, and command higher prices on average than yellow babies. They are frequently marked with yellow or white cross bars or triangles. Sometimes these are large and bold, and sometimes they are reduced in size or number, and they are usually outlined with dark borders. In some neonates the dorsal markings are broken up into small fractured shapes.

A spectacular gold and rust colored neonate with white spots present. (GM-03-06)

There may be dark or light-colored spots and bars in between the larger markings.

A popular phase of yellow baby that has shown up in recent years is the "blaze" form. Blaze babies have a reddish wash of color down the dorsal area, in varying degrees of width and intensity. While such babies are very attractive, there is evidence that the trait itself doesn't mean anything in particular about how the animal will color up as an adult. Another fairly new neonate variety is "patternless", and babies of both yellow and dark phases can have greatly reduced dorsal or lateral markings and may appear almost one solid color. "Calico Junior" (GM-99-09) was a brown example of this baby phase, and my 50% Lemon Tree offspring have had greatly reduced patterns too.

It is interesting to note that the baby colors of hatchling chondros do seem to be very dependant on the original baby colors of the parents and appear to reflect the influence of dominant and recessive genes. Yellow hatchlings are the most common, and for many years it was considered

Maroon babies typically have white or yellow dorsal markings, and these can be very bold or reduced in size.

unusual to hatch out any maroon babies (Walsh, pers. com. 1997). This was most likely due to the acquisition of founder stock by early U.S. breeders that were yellow as juveniles. Like brown eyes in humans, yellow is the dominant trait in baby chondros. As breeders began to utilize adults that had been dark babies, more dark offspring began to show up. It has now been demonstrated that clutches of all dark babies usually result from parents that were both dark as youngsters. Clutches from mixed parentage often contain both yellow and dark babies. There is no evidence of sexual dimorphism related to baby color phases.

Brown babies can be almost black. Some have barely discernable blotches or crossbars. The author hatched this beauty in 2002.

One of the most frequent questions I am asked by prospective customers is about the relationship between baby color phases and the final results of the adult color change. I can state with certainty that the *genetics of the parents in particular, and the entire family tree in general*, have much more to do with the appearance of an adult chondro than its baby color. There are a few common beliefs about the relationship between neonate colors and the adult colors that result from them. It is often thought that only yellow babies develop into high yellow adults, and that maroon or brown offspring are more prone to produce unusual forms. There is a grain of truth involved with these theories. For example, the Lemon Tree bloodline is known to produce only yellow offspring. However, I have high yellow adults in my collection that came from maroon babies. The fact that many high-end morph breeders in the U.S. prefer to breed for dark babies has contributed to the feeling that all high-end adults come from dark offspring, but again this is not always true.

There has been some speculation as to the possible correlation between baby patterns and coloration, and the racial purity of the parents. European breeders, who have always focused more on race than "locality" in

This attractive chondro was a "blaze" baby produced by Trooper Walsh, but the parents contributed to the adult colors much more than the baby phase did.

their breeding projects, favor the perspective that each race tends to produce babies with patterns unique to that race. While I admit that I don't have the depth of experience with chondro race breeding that some Europeans do, I haven't really seen a clear distinction between offspring from the Aru and mainland forms. What I have observed is wide variability in the appearance of all offspring, as well as neonates that closely match illustrations of supposed race-specific colors and patterns but in fact have no known relationship to a particular race. In some instances my neonates exhibit characteristics that are supposedly associated with one race but are in reality from parents that more closely resemble the descriptions of another race. In fact, the experiences of many U.S. breeders working with specific forms, seems to directly contradict the views of others. For example, there is wide agreement by U.S. breeders that pure specimens of the Aru race produce only yellow offspring. European breeders not only report dark Aru neonates, but also feel that these offspring exhibit a unique broken pattern. There are several possibilities that might explain this apparent contradiction, but the important point here is that one must be cautious when ascribing unique baby traits to specific race or locality animals.

This Biak-type juvenile exhibits typical orange-red and yellow coloration and bold markings.

A frequent exception is certain offspring of the Biak Race. While I haven't been able to make any consistent observations about yellow hatchlings of this race, the maroon babies often have a distinct look to them, with large, rounded, yellow or orange dorsal markings. These offspring are notoriously slow to fully change into the adult colors.

Ontogenic Color Change

Perhaps the most fascinating element of raising chondros is watching the yearlings go through their color and pattern changes. There are no rules here, and literally anything can happen. Some animals change quickly, even overnight. Some may take several years to fully assume their adult appearance. Some are rather drab as they exchange baby colors for adult ones and others may temporarily look like the autumn forest ablaze with color. Predictably, yellow neonates have a different progression of changes compared to dark babies. However, there are some generalities that can be made, and that apply to the majority of specimens.

On average, young chondros begin to show color changes at about six months to a year in age. Yellow neonates usually begin the development of adult colors with the appearance of a few flecks of green on their bodies, and sometimes around the nostrils. These green scales continue to spread and grow and soon the animal has a green wash of color over most of its body. This change can happen very

This photo shows the beginning of the color change in a yellow hatchling, with green scales developing.

quickly, but often takes place over several weeks or even a few months. The green can be bright or dull, even slightly gray looking. If the animal is destined to have white dorsal markings as an adult, such as specimens from the Aru race, this is usually the first color to develop, sometimes even before the green begins to come in. The white markings don't contrast well with the yellow body and may be a little difficult to see at

first. Some collectors have observed the white markings continuing to develop into the second and third year of growth.

Many yellow babies of the Sorong type have red dorsal markings at hatching that will turn gray as the animal changes colors. These gray-blue markings often develop into pretty

This yearling chondro was a dark brown baby, produced by the author from blue parents. Animal courtesy of Thomas Phillips.

blue markings as the animal fully matures, often with a purple intermediate stage. It can take two to three years before the blue fully develops and even then these markings can look purple or gray in poor lighting, such as indoor florescent lights. In fact, all chondros will look their best when viewed outdoors. This is the ultimate "full spectrum" lighting, and the effect can often be somewhat duplicated indoors using full spectrum lights.

Dark babies start their color changes most often by a general lightening up of the body color. Very

This maroon hatchling is showing the typical greenish color and blue dorsal markings often seen during the color change. Animal produced by the author.

dark babies can adopt a light brown, slightly greenish color; maroon babies usually go through an orange phase as they lighten up. Dark stripes and diamond outlines often turn blue, and yellow dorsal markings often lose their brilliance and fill in with blue or gray, although some specimens keep the bright yellow into adulthood. Some maroon or brown babies slowly change to some shade of light or dark green, but others go through a period of intense coloration that is exciting and beautiful to watch. This is one of the reasons some keepers favor maroon babies.

Examples of the Biak race frequently take much longer to complete the color change than most other chondros, whether wild type or designer bred. As was mentioned earlier, these changes can be temporarily dramatic, leading the observer to conclude that something really special is taking place. However, these specimens characteristically go on to become typical adult Biak specimens that conform to the description of the race given in the previous chapter.

Biak juveniles are notoriously slow to undergo their ontogenic color change, and the colors of yearlings and young adults can not be trusted to represent the final appearance. This animal (GM-02-04) is five days short of its first birthday.

A common question regarding the color change is how to know when a particular animal is done changing. This is especially on the mind of those watching the offspring from designer morph parents develop. I will make some comments about the specific color changes often associated with designer morphs in the next section, but as a generality, most young chondros will go through a stage where change is occurring most rapidly, and then it will slow down and taper off. Usually, the color change is mostly complete by the time three months or so have passed without any significant changes taking place, once the initial changes have slowed or stopped. I have also noticed a loose correlation between how quickly the onset of the color change occurs, and how long it will last. Animals that experience a rapid onset of color change often complete those changes in a relatively short time, and when they slow down, you have what you are going to end up with. When color changes begin very slowly, the completion of them takes longer on average. Most specimens of chondros tend to undergo subtle changes as they pass through the stages of young adulthood into a mature animal. But in my experience observing hundreds of chondros, you usually have a good idea about how the animal will finally look, once you have had three months without any substantial changes, after the initial color change stabilizes.

Color change is not dependant on the environment, from what I can observe, but is clearly tied in with growth rates. Chondros that are "late bloomers" in terms of eating and becoming established as hatchlings, will change colors well behind the schedule of their average clutch mates, and right on time with their own growth rate. Because of this fact, the time frames mentioned above are relative to average feeding and growth rates. I do not believe that the timing, rapidity, or ultimate results of yearling color changes are affected by temperature, cage environment, or exposure to other external stimuli, except for how any of these may affect the growth rate. In other words, I don't think there is any way to manipulate the color change of individual animals by exposing them to external factors. My feeling is that the DNA of each animal determines everything about how it will look and how it will get there. These comments apply specifically to CB chondros. There has been some discussion about environmental factors influencing the appearance of wild caught specimens of certain geographic races. There may be something to this, and there are known cases where specific kinds of CB reptiles or amphibians look different than their WC counterparts due to habitat or food differences. However, there is no hard evidence of this with chondros.

Thus far, I have not speculated about the actual mechanics of GTP color changes. A lot of theories have been postulated, some making sense and others seemingly a bit far-fetched. I don't think anybody completely understands just how or why young chondros change colors. Many theories about why neonates are colored so brilliantly have been offered, as have ideas about why they are found in both gold and maroon phases. In fact, color change isn't limited to young animals; gravid female chondros are known to frequently undergo color changes that may or may not be permanent. Some color morphs may be explained by the absence of a normal pigment. For example, high yellow animals may be lacking the pigment that is responsible for blue. This blue pigment, when combined with yellow, might produce the common green adult color. This theory is further strengthened by the evidence that gravid high yellow females often tend to turn pale or white rather than blue, as is usually the case with gravid females undergoing color change. However, there are far too many variables, color combinations, and strange color developments, to explain all of them so simply. It is probable that the presence or absence of several kinds of pigmented skin cells, and the combinations they produce, are responsible for the fantastic colors these animals display.

Descriptions of Designer Color Morphs

Now that we have discussed chondro genetics, baby color phases, and the ontogenic color change, it is appropriate to describe some of the designer color morphs being bred in captivity. The number of color variations in wild populations, combined with the extreme variability of the species within both wild and captive bred bloodlines, make GTPs perfect candidates for the development of some beautiful and unusual color morphs. While some have expressed a moral problem with breeding specimens that don't appear to be of the same race, and have even gone so far as to suggest that offspring from parents of mixed ancestry are "hybrids", I feel nothing but awe for some of these incredible animals. It seems pretty arrogant to bestow second-class status to such animals when the origin of the founder stock for the supposed racially pure animals isn't even known in the majority of cases! Such bias is purely human, and personal; there is no moral absolute dictating which color form or type of chondro is better than another. For more about this issue, please see the comments in the previous chapter regarding the breeding of racially pure animals.

High Yellow

Perhaps the original "designer" chondro morph is high yellow. There is something glorious and breathtaking about seeing an adult chondro that is covered with bright yellow scales. Many chondros have some yellow on them, with the notable exception of typical Aru stock. It was only natural that sooner or later breeders would attempt to reinforce this trait by selective breeding. Strangely enough, the best high yellow specimens come from bloodlines that produced spontaneous yellow adults from green parents, rather than from culling and crossing adults with increasing amounts of yellow on them. There are a couple of well-known bloodlines that have demonstrated the ability to produce high yellow offspring. Perhaps none is more potent or better known than the Lemon Tree line,

"Matrix" (JH-99) is a spectacular and unusual high yellow male in the author's collection. Produced by Jeff Hudson.

originating from a California breeder named Tim Turmezie. In fact, some people view the name "Lemon Tree" and high yellow chondros as being synonymous, although the LT designation rightfully belongs specifically to animals produced by this bloodline.

Turmezie works primarily with colubrids, but in the early nineties he purchased a group of three captive bred neonate chondros from Doug Price. Price hatched the three babies from clutches produced by breeding some wild caught adults that were reported to be PNG in origin. The three neonates were not related (not siblings), but the relationship of the parents is not known. One of the three neonates acquired by Turmezie developed into a gorgeous yellow male with dark green random scales. The male was about 75% yellow, with a green crown, and some random white flowers scattered on the body. This male became the founder of the Lemon Tree bloodline. The other two animals turned out to be females; one with some yellow speckling and the other a blue animal. Turmezie crossed the male with both females, producing several clutches beginning in 1995. Some of these offspring developed into beautiful high yellow adults, including some almost solid yellow specimens. Others had a mix of green and yellow, and some were mostly green. These second

"Happy Jack", a spectacular male Lemon Tree chondro in the author's collection, produced by Tim Turmezie.

generation offspring demonstrated the potency of the Lemon Tree bloodline and helped define the characteristics unique to it.

These include bright lemon yellow and beautiful forest green coloration, a tendency for the head to have a crown of contrasting color, offspring that stop developing green at an early stage in the color change process, and that are always yellow as hatchlings. One undesirable attribute of this bloodline is frequent fertility problems, especially between related specimens.

Ophiological Services (OS), mentioned in the chapter about chondro

"Lilly" (TT-95), a gorgeous Lemon Tree female in the author's collection. The tendency of Lemons and other yellow females to turn pale or white after pregnancy can be seen.

"Chiquita" (GM-99-01) is one of two 50% Lemons held back from a 1999 clutch produced by the author.

history, also has a high yellow bloodline associated with their name. OS has produced some very beautiful high yellow animals, and this bloodline is more variable and seems to be less potent than the Lemon Tree bloodline. This is probably due to a more diverse genetic pool in the founder animals. Some OS high yellow specimens have brilliant yellows and bright greens, while others display pale pastel colors that are very different than those of the LT animals. Like the Lemon Tree line, the OS high yellow line has produced a few outstanding adults that have a high percentage of yellow. Unlike Lemon Trees, the OS line tends to enjoy a higher fertility rate.

Tony Nicoli, another arboreal breeder from the southern United States, has also produced a number of high yellow specimens. However, most of the Nicoli founder stock was OS in origin (Bessette, pers. com.) and many collectors don't make much of a distinction between the two lines. In fact, some of the founder stock for the line is not completely documented as coming from OS originally (Hudson, pers. com.). Nicoli sold his collection of chondros in 2000 and no longer works with the species, focusing instead on the Emerald Tree Boa, a completely unrelated species from South America. Other breeders have produced spontaneous high yellow specimens from non-yellow adults, including Jeff Hudson (who

"Grace" (GM-99-04), another of the author's 1999 50% Lemons.

purchased the Nicoli collection) and Jack Sadovnik. Both of these individuals, as well as others, are currently working to establish new high yellow bloodlines based on new founder animals. It has been claimed that both the LT and OS lines (including the Nicoli animals) do not have Biak blood involved in them. This seems to be contradicted by the evidence, for many specimens I have examined from both lines tend to have characteristic Biak heads with long noses and long, pointed tails. However, some specimens do conform more closely to PNG head and tail

"Oz" (EB-98) is a spectacular high yellow male produced by Ophiological Services and owned by the author.

descriptions.

The question has arisen more than once as to the genetic compatibility of the LT line and the OS line, and if crossing specimens from these lines would yield good results. (The alleles responsible for high yellow in one bloodline might not necessarily correspond to the alleles in a different bloodline, even though both adults look yellow. See the genetics discussion earlier in this chapter.) Breeder Buddy

This outstanding yellow female was originally produced by OS and was sold to Nicoli after being purchased by a third party in a NJ pet store! Animal courtesy of Jeff Hudson.

If racial descriptions mean anything, then some of these high yellow animals have Biak blood in them. Note the long snout on this animal.

Goetzger helped to resolve that question when he successfully bred a LT male to an OS high yellow female in 2001. In an outstanding success for a first-time

"Hershey" (BG-01-10), one of two Lemon Tree x OS Yellow offspring in the author's collection produced by Buddy Goetzger.

breeder, he produced a clutch of offspring that developed into some outstanding young adults, including some high yellow animals. I have two of these offspring and they are both gorgeous, but only one could be

"Rusty" (BG-01-04) was named for his brick-red baby color. Lemon x OS, produced by Buddy Goetzger.

characterized as "high yellow". Goetzger's success did not conclusively prove that all LT x OS pairings will produce high-end results, but it certainly showed the potential of combining the two bloodlines. It also demonstrated that the belief that only yellow offspring develop into high yellow adults was incorrect, an assumption that is most likely linked to the fact that Lemon Tree offspring are known to always be yellow.

Is this a "high yellow" chondro? Not by any serious measure, but this type of animal is often seen represented as such in on-line classified ads. This animal is "SOB" (Son of Barnose, GM-98-13) and is a Biak outcross.

There has been an abuse of the term "high yellow" by both commercial dealers and private sellers. How much yellow is required before an animal can be honestly represented as "high" yellow? That is a question that can only be answered by each individual. Like the U.S. Supreme Court Justice who said of pornography, "I know it when I see it, and in this case this isn't it", I have seen a lot of animals advertised as high yellow that came nowhere near a reasonable example of this morph. Especially prone to exaggeration (or dishonesty) are those selling half-changed Biaks, which often hold some yellow for a long time before losing it to the typical adult colors, which are mostly green. Perhaps ignorance of this fact could have been used as an excuse some years ago, but with the information revolution brought on by the Internet, the truth about "yellow" Biaks is now well-know. Nevertheless, the deceptive ads keep coming. True high yellow chondros are quite valuable and the best individuals can command prices well over $10,000.

High Blue

This beautiful morph is also an extremely popular one with collectors. While blue adults may not have the same initial "shock" effect on the viewer as other, more vibrantly colored morphs do, there is something

"My Song" (TW-98-25) is one of the best high blue females to be found anywhere. She is in the author's collection and has been blue since her ontogenic color change.

very classy and appealing about these sky-colored beauties. Perhaps this is because blue seems appropriate for these tree dwelling pythons; wild-collected blue specimens are occasionally found, and the color does not have the "artificial" look to it that some feel other designer morphs do. The blue colors on adult chondros can range from grayish blue all the way to bright turquoise. The best specimens seem to glow, and can be spotted resting on a branch from across a large room.

There is a confusing element to this morph, and one that is misunderstood by many chondro lovers. This is the fact that there are two types of blue chondros; females that have undergone a color shift during breeding and pregnancy, and chondros of either sex that have an unusual quantity of blue pigment. While both forms are referred to as high blue, or simply "blue chondros", they are not the same thing, and may not necessarily be genetically compatible. Let us look first at the color-shifted blue females.

When female chondros are cycled for breeding and begin to develop egg follicles, they frequently undergo a color change as a part of the symptoms of impending ovulation. Not all females do this and not all of them that do turn blue, but the phenomenon is well-documented. The onset of the color change usually coincides with the refusal of food and a swelled appearance caused by the ripening follicles in the ovaries. The shade and depth of blue can vary from an aqua color to deep turquoise. Some females will have a decidedly gray cast and some can be sky blue. This color change has

"Aquagirl" (TW-93-12) is a fine example of a "hormonal" blue female that turned permanently blue after pregnancy.

long been assumed to be hormonal in nature, and such blue female specimens are often referred to as "hormonal blue". This blue color is not exclusive to females developing follicles; the same symptom can be seen in chondros with a tumor of the kidney or ovary (Barker, pers. com.). Some females will return to the normal green adult color following egg deposition (and after incubation if maternal incubation is allowed), some will regress to an aqua color, and some will keep the blue color permanently. Most females that keep an aqua color after the first breeding will keep more of the blue after the second, and will become permanently blue after the third. Females from PNG origins seem most prone to this color change, and blue Aru females

"Angel" is one of the author's females that took on a decidedly bluish tone following her second pregnancy. She is seen here recovering from egg laying a week prior.

are also fairly common. Blue examples of the Biak race are very uncommon, in my experience.

Animals with a high amount of blue pigment on the dorsal and lateral areas of the body make up the second type of blue morph adult. Many chondros have some blue on them, especially those typical of the Sorong race, with their blue dorsal stripes and triangular markings. While these animals can be very attractive, they are not included in this morph description. True high blue chondros have blue over much or all of the body, not just nice blue markings. This blue color is found on the skin between the scales, as well as on the scales themselves, and can also be seen on the upper and lower labials as well. Good specimens of this morph are not common, far less common than high yellow animals. Even the best animals usually have some green on them, usually light and faded, and in the places where there were baby markings such as dorsal triangles and head stripes.

Tim Morris of Maryland produced what is generally considered to be the best-known example of this morph. Tim was given a smallish twin neonate chondro as a gift, and this animal went on to sire a clutch for Morris that produced his famous blue male (Walsh, pers. com.). Although no longer owned by Morris, his name is still associated with

The well-known "Morris" blue male. This wonderful chondro is responsible for generating much of the initial enthusiasm for selectively bred blue chondros. Animal and photo courtesy of John Holland.

this magnificent male. Now owned by collector John Holland, this male has been bred several times to various females, including his own mother. Some very attractive animals have been produced from this line, including animals with a lot of nice blue coloration. I have not yet seen any of the offspring match the electric blue of the original male. While on breeding loan to Trooper Walsh in 2002, the male sired two clutches that have great potential.

"Aquaman" (TW-95-05) This blue male is one of the best examples of this morph. He is a proven blue offspring producer from the author's breeding colony.

A blue male in my own collection is another fine example of this morph. "Aquaman" (TW-95-05) has sired several blue offspring with three different females, including two hormonal blue females as well as a captive bred Sorong type. The 2000 Sorong clutch produced an incredible blue male that may end up exceeding the color of the sire. "Blue Max" (GM-00-18), is now in the collection of Greg and Michelle Gibbs. Also at the time of writing, a young dark brown juvenile sired by "Aquaman" with "Aquagirl" in 2001 ("Blue Frost", GM-01-30) is already developing strong blue pigment and is showing great promise. A Walsh animal in my collection, "My Song" (TW-98-25, see photo on page 74), is a beautiful high blue female

"Blue Max" (GM-00-18) is an outstanding example of a selectively bred blue chondro.

"Blue Frost" (GM-01-30), produced by the author in 2001, is an outstanding genetic blue chondro. Both parents are blue.

that developed all her blue prior to being bred. Another female, "Pepper" (AZ-96-14), produced in 1996 by Al Zulich, also had an unusual amount of blue coloration prior to her first breeding. (See her photo in the "mite phase" section of this chapter.)

I'm enthusiastic about working with females that are not hormonal specimens, and that developed into high blue morph animals as a natural part of their ontogenic color change. I feel they may present better chances for producing blue morph offspring when paired with blue males. Hormonal blue females are very beautiful and may produce female offspring that will turn hormonally blue themselves after experiencing one or more pregnancies. (See the photo of "Alice" (GM-99-42) in the chapter on Captive History.)

However, I have not seen conclusive evidence indicating that crossing a blue male with a hormonal female gives better results than crossing such a male with a normal female. I have done both, and to date outstanding offspring have resulted from using both types of females.

Is this a "high blue" chondro? Time will tell whether this young female (TW-01) will develop into a true high blue morph. The author has seen chondros with less blue on them than this one advertised as "blue screamers".

Plenty of green adults have also resulted from breeding blue adults together in several collections. The results from breeding my "true blue" females will be most interesting in the continued development of this morph. One thing is sure; this morph is not as established or consistent as the high yellow morph is, although certainly progress is being made.

This attractive Sorong-type (GM-00-21) will take several years to fully develop its blue colors. This is not a high blue chondro.

Blue chondros were considered rare some years ago, and the difference between the two types was not commonly understood. It is now known that hormonal blue females, while beautiful and desirable, are not all that uncommon. Truly high blue examples of the second type are among the most sought after of designer chondro morphs and can command very high prices. This has led, predictably, to the same kinds of abuse, exaggeration, and hype that often accompany ads for high yellow animals. Again, while personal taste and opinion is involved in deciding what is "high" blue, it can be truly amazing what passes for a high blue chondro on some on-line classifieds boards or swap meet vendor's tables. I once saw a solid green adult chondro at a Pottstown, Pennsylvania reptile show labeled as "true blue". I was both amused and irritated by this, because I originally coined that term to distinguish real high blue animals from those that were the object of sales hype. I included hormonal females in the "true blue" group at the time, because of the frequency with which chondros with any amount of blue on them were being marketed as "high blue". However, the term has evolved so that many collectors today use it to distinguish ontogenic blue adults from hormonal blue females. I consider adults from both groups to be highly desirable and valuable.

In my experience, both Sorong type specimens and true blue animals often take a number of years to fully develop their blue colors. These chondros always look their best when seen in natural outdoor lighting, or under a good full spectrum florescent light. Incidentally, there is no recorded instance of blue neonates hatching. You cannot tell from looking at a baby whether it will be a blue adult or not. As always, the parents will greatly determine the color characteristics of the offspring, and parents with proven, documented, past results are the best bet when seeking to acquire unchanged babies that have potential for good blue coloration down the road.

Calico Chondros

Calico chondros exhibit a beautiful and unique blend of colors, and speckled and blotched patterns. Although there are at least two different color types, the Yellow and the Chocolate, the speckled pattern comprised of many different colors is what distinguishes the morph as something different from anything else. The visual effect of the many individually pigmented scales is similar to viewing the pixels on a computer monitor, up close. Calico chondros have up to nine readily distinguishable colors, including orange and yellow-orange, light yellow, dark and lime green, chocolate and reddish brown, black, white, aqua, blue, and mustard. The bloodline has also demonstrated a strong tendency for the head color to stand out in contrast to the neck, the latter often showing colors and patterns unique from the rest of the body.

The calico project is one that is very dear to my heart, because I am the developer of it. For the record, I did not invent the term "calico", nor am I the first to apply it to a reptile color morph. Probably the calico house cat is the most familiar application of

"The Computer Chondro" (TW-93-05) is the founder male for the calico project, and one of the most beautiful chondros ever produced.

the word to an animal, and reptile morphs of the same name do not share the tri-color genetics or the gender specifics with the feline version. (Almost all calico cats are females and have the same three colors.) There are calico morphs described for Burmese, Reticulated, and Royal (Ball) Pythons, among others. These morphs are not the same as calico chondros, and do not share the

These photos show the diversity of colors, pixelated patterns, and head and neck colors that stand out from the body that characterize calico chondros.

Founder male showing full head, neck, and body details of color and pattern.

same characteristics with them.

The founder animal for this project was produced in 1993 as a brown baby from a January clutch, hatched by breeder Trooper Walsh from normal parents. As the young chondro began its color change, it soon became apparent that something different was happening. The chondro developed a yellow body color, but was heavily specked with other colors including light green, dark green, black, yellow, yellow-orange, light blue, aqua, and white. Added to the interesting and attractive mix of colors was the unique way they were speckled and splattered evenly on the animal from head to tail. The only exception in this evenness of distribution was that the head was more or less green, with yellow-orange beginning on the neck immediately behind the lobes. In some places, individual scales of distinct colors occupied adjacent locations on the body, and in others, scales of similar colors formed small patches. The whole

"Calico Junior" (GM-99-09) is perhaps the most unusual captive produced designer chondro in the world and verified that the calico traits were inheritable.

effect was similar to the grainy breakup of color on a computer monitor when viewed close up. I purchased this animal as a twenty-month-old male. At the time, I think everybody assumed he was a one-of-a-kind oddball. I nicknamed him "The Computer Chondro" due to the pixel-like pattern.

By lucky coincidence, over half a year earlier I had purchased a normal female that was a sibling to this male. I decided to breed them in an effort to concentrate the possibilities for producing another calico animal, and after three attempts I succeeded in getting a viable clutch. Only three

"Calico Junior" as a day-old hatchling. He was one of the best patternless dark babies I have ever seen.

83

offspring survived (that is part of another story) but one of them, a very dark baby with few markings, showed unusual patterning and coloration at a year of age, and developed into the second known calico male, "Calico Junior" (GM-99-09). Junior has the same pixilated pattern and distinct

"Lemongirl" (TW-94-144), dam of the April 2001 calico clutch that has produced several very special offspring. She must be seen alive to truly appreciate her beauty.

head and neck differentiation as his father, but his many colors seem to be the reverse of the founder male. Where that animal has yellow as the

This fantastic calico female (GM-01-15) was produced by the author in 2001. Animal courtesy of Thomas Phillips.

primary ground color, Junior has dark chocolate brown. Green, yellow, red-orange, yellow-orange, aqua, light blue, and pea green can all be seen on him. While I was ecstatic to have produced such a beautiful and unique animal, I was equally enthusiastic to have demonstrated that the calico pattern was a heritable trait. Junior's two surviving siblings

These two calico specimens (GM-01-06, top and GM-01-08, bottom) are examples of what I hope to establish as a chocolate variation of the morph, much like "Calico Junior".

(GM-01-02), top, and (GM-01-12), bottom, are two females I held back from the 2001 calico clutch.

were pretty animals, but looked nothing like him or the sire. In the fall of 2000 I bred the founder male to a beautiful, mostly unrelated yellow, green and blue female, and a clutch was produced that began to hatch on April Fool's Day, 2001.

Eighteen offspring were produced, but not all survived due to a bacterial infection in the egg yolk that claimed several young when they were a few weeks old. About a dozen survived, and these offspring have developed into outstanding animals. One female in particular has turned out to be spectacular. This animal, owned by Tomm Phillips, will hopefully make a large contribution to the development of the yellow form of this morph. A female holdback in my collection exhibits dark colors similar to Calico Junior, but admittedly

"Miss Kitty" (GM-01-14) is another spectacular female from the author's 2001 calico clutch. She is in the collection of Janet Hickner, who supplied this photograph.

with less variety, and less dark pigment. She will likely become the founder female for developing the chocolate form of the calico morph.

"Rosina" (TW-98-26) is another Walsh production that I just had to have. She will hopefully contribute her calico-like pattern to the project in the near future.

A chocolate male was also produced and is in a private collection. I have two other females from this clutch that are showing great promise as well. I am tracking the results of a few other animals from the clutch, and an animal owned by Janet Hickner of Indiana has developed into a yellow beauty. I am not aware of any other clutch produced from designer morph parents that has produced the consistently outstanding results seen in this one.

As with other valuable morphs, there have been those who have attempted to profit from the demand for the real thing by making false claims for animals that bear no resemblance to the actual bloodline. Half-changed Biaks are the most frequent animals advertised as "calico" in classified ads. Also, chocolate calicos such as "Calico Junior" are not the same as the melanistic (dark) specimens sometimes seen, nor are they associated with black-speckled highland localities.

Occasionally, other unusual chondros will be called "calico", but the term is not a catch-all for any oddball or unusual chondros that may show up. While I don't hold a patent for using the word to describe this morph, it is professional and ethical to respect the use of a term describing a unique combination of traits, when the person who developed the line gives it that name. For example, there are a lot of high yellow chondros out there, yet most of the chondro community respects the use of the term "Lemon Tree" as uniquely referring to the line started by Tim Turmezie. Calicos are what they are… a unique combination of pattern and colors unlike anything else in the world of designer bred GTPs. Admittedly still in the developmental stage, the future of this morph looks very promising, especially in light of the results of the 2001 breeding. Two calico pairings are planned for the 2003 fall and winter breeding period.

"Mite Phase"

This term was coined by a young keeper named John Romano, to describe animals with black speckling. The name isn't popular with everyone, possibly due to the rather negative association with that bane of reptile collections, the snake mite. Also, strictly speaking, a "phase" is a temporary stage of development, not a permanent morph. However, the name stuck and has come into wide usage, so we all had better get used to it! Mite phase animals can be heavily peppered with black, have reduced speckling, limited even to skin pigment between the scales, or the speckling can disappear altogether as the animal matures. This happens more frequently than breeders would like, making the ownership of a mite phase animal somewhat in doubt until it reaches maturity. Even heavily marked yearlings can lose the black flecks entirely by the time they are two or three years old. However, such animals may still pass on the trait to youngsters. In fact, I have a green male that never had any mite phase coloration on him even as a changeling, yet he has produced several nice mite phase offspring. This trait does seem to be fairly potent within a bloodline, and often if one parent has or had the trait it will show up in a number of the offspring. Extreme examples are very attractive and desirable, especially when combined with a blue body color.

"Pepper" (AZ-96) is an outstanding "mite phase" female produced by Al Zulich and obtained by the author as a hatchling.

Other Color Varieties

There are other color varieties that have captured the eye of collectors recently, and a few breeders are working to reinforce these qualities. However, they have not been sufficiently established at the time of writing to qualify as recognized morphs with heritable traits, although it is probable that some of them will in the future. These include:

Mustard… this is a variety with the color of brown hot dog mustard, and varies between a drab yellow

A nice example of a Mustard chondro produced by Jim Devolder from Nicoli stock. Photo courtesy of Steve Gordon.

and an olive green. While not a favorite with many collectors, mustard chondros do have their fans, and there have been a few attempts at breeding this color. So far, I'm not aware of any documented mustard offspring, but certainly it is only a matter of time before this color is more established.

High contrast male "Kermit", produced by Winslow Murdoch and in the collection of Thomas Phillips.

High Contrast…
these are animals with several colors that stand out from each other, such as green, yellow, and blue. Some of these animals can be very attractive, and can command as high a price as some of the more established designer morphs.

High White… predictably, these are most often high-end examples of the Aru race. It seems odd that the amount of white on chondros has not shown as strong a tendency to increase with selective breeding, as have other color traits. I am aware of a few breeders who are working to develop high white bloodlines of Aru types, which will consistently produce a percentage of high white offspring. One of these, a breeder experienced with multiple generations of selective breeding, estimates that in any given clutch the high white expression is between 15 and 30 percent (Rouille, pers. com.). There is evidence that males are frequently more heavily marked with white than are the females, but this is not always the case. The high white Yapen form of the Biak race seems even less established in captivity than are high white Arus.

Key Lime… a relatively new color recognition, this variety is characterized by a solid green body with no white or other colors present. Some breeders have questioned the actual tone and brightness of the green as being a distinguishable and consistent variant. This is due to the fact that a few obviously overexposed digital photos of normal green chondros have been represented as being of "key lime" specimens. Nevertheless, there are some breeders, such as Rico Walder of Signal Herpetoculture, that are interested in developing this color variety, and it may well prove to be a trait that can be strengthened with selective breeding.

Paradox... this is a new project being developed by Damon Salceies, mentioned earlier as one of those working with locality specific Merauke chondros and the producer of the first living albino chondro (see below). The paradox animals originate from Houston Zoo stock and are noted for high yellow and blue combinations with an unusual blotched pattern. These are an extreme deviation from naturally occurring morphs, but are fantastic looking, and there is early evidence to indicate that the traits are heritable.

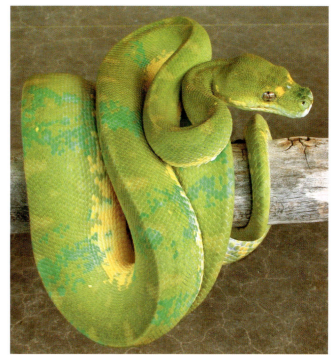

This highly unusual "Paradox" chondro is part of a group originating from Houston Zoo stock. Photo courtesy of Damon Salceies.

Albino Chondros

When writing of this book commenced, no one had yet produced a living albino chondro in captivity, nor were there verifiable reports of any being observed or captured in the wild. Speculation about the possibilities of the first captive bred albino chondro is something that has long stirred the imagination and interest of most people in the chondro community.

There have been a couple of questionable reports of albino hatchlings. One of these that has gotten a lot of press was a photo published on the VPI web site by Dave Barker. The image is of a dead, under-pigmented neonate that died nearly full-term. The image was published as part of a web contest to find the animal on the site, and Barker later admitted that the animal was not an albino, and even confessed to coloring the eye of

The first captive bred albino chondro. Photo courtesy of Damon Salceies.

the animal to make it look more albinistic. The photo has caused a lot of questions and has stirred the interest in albino GTPs. There have been one or two other photos published that claim to be of albino hatchlings. In each case the animals clearly appear to be dead, under-pigmented, nearly full-term neonates. The full pigmentation is the last thing to develop in hatchling chondros, in the last few days of incubation, and animals that fail to survive and hatch often look pale and much like an albino might. Trooper Walsh reported hatching a true albino, with red eyes and tongue, which failed to survive twenty-four hours. Unfortunately, there are no photos available of the animal (Walsh, pers. com. 1999).

In an ironic twist to the Barker "albino" photo, two baby chondros produced by Tracy Barker in 1996, from locality-specific imported Merauke parents, ended up making history as the pair that produced the first known living albino chondro. Damon Salceies, a breeder of locality *alterna*, purchased some of the 1996 Barker clutch in order to work with some verified locality chondros. A pair of these siblings produced a clutch for him that hatched in January 2002, and included two albino yellow neonates. One of these animals succumbed to a bacterial skin infection, but the other thrived, and Mr. Salceies made his announcement

The albino along with a normal sibling. Note the red eye and pale lavender markings on the albino. Photo courtesy of Damon Salceies.

about the remarkable event at the National Breeders Expo in Daytona, Florida in August of 2002. Damon graciously called me to let me know of the upcoming announcement, and his post on the ChondroForum about the albino set a new forum record for replies and hits to a single topic. His photos of the animal in this book are the first to be published in print. At the time of this writing, the albino is just beginning the first hints of its ontogenic color change, and there is much excitement and speculation about how it will ultimately develop as an adult.

A few people have expressed disappointment that the albino isn't white, or that it doesn't look like they expected. A couple persons have even suggested that the animal is not all that valuable because it isn't outrageously different from the normal siblings. This kind of thinking is very short sighted and fails to grasp what the production of the first albino chondro will certainly mean for designer breeding. Each race and captive color morph will likely produce a different form of albino when outcrossed. These will take years to develop and establish, but what an exciting event each hatching will be! With other, far less marketable species of first-time albino pythons selling for many thousands of dollars, albino chondros represent a substantial and long-term investment. Other

The albino and a sibling as yearlings, just beginning the ontogenic color change. Photo courtesy of Damon Salceies.

owners of 1996 Barker Merauke offspring are excited about the possibility that they may own specimens that are het for albino. Trooper Walsh produced a clutch of Merauke out-crossed offspring in the spring of 2001, sired by his male from the Barker clutch. As an owner of one of these offspring, I can entertain the small chance that I too might possibly possess a het male! I share Damon Salceies' hope that the chondro community will appreciate these wonderful and unique animals for what they are, and hold their high economic value as a secondary measure of worth.

Chapter 5. Chondro Myths and Misunderstandings

"I shall try to correct errors when shown to be errors, and I shall adopt new views so fast as they shall appear to be true views."

Abraham Lincoln

GTPs are mysterious creatures, and can be inconsistent in their behaviors, personalities, and habits. This combination of factors and the tendency of humans to draw conclusions based on incomplete evidence, has led to some common misconceptions about them. As these assumptions get repeated they develop into mindsets and myths. The Internet has been especially problematic in the spreading of misinformation around the world; but it has also made the correcting of some of these myths easier as well. Some of the following myths have been made popular by those who believe what they have observed in a few specimens to be true for all. It must be stated that when seeking to discover the facts about chondros, large sample sizes must be used as the baseline for comparing data. *Too often, firm conclusions are made by those with limited experience, or from observing too small a number of animals.* Exceptions occur to every rule, especially with these snakes, and errors can be made when the exception is presented as the rule.

The following are some common and frequently misunderstood claims about chondros, along with a brief explanation of the facts. Most of these topics are covered in detail elsewhere in this book. This list is by no means exhaustive, but does cover all the common claims one frequently hears. The topics are arranged to address biological issues first, followed by husbandry and health concerns.

Myth # 1: "GTPs are irritable, snappy reptiles that can't be handled without danger of being bitten."

This belief has its roots in the days when most chondros were wild caught. Such specimens are notoriously irritable. The fact is, most captive bred adult chondros are relatively calm animals and can be safely free-handled during the daylight hours. There are exceptions, with a few really psychotic specimens around, and also some that are dog tame. My observation is that most prefer to be left alone, and I don't make a practice of handling mine unless there is a need to, but many keepers do enjoy handling their animals. Neonate chondros are normally quite snappy, and even if they are not, it is a good practice to avoid handling them prior to a year of age, due to the fragility of the spine. Most CB chondros will begin to tame down on their own at about twelve to eighteen months of age with little or no taming required, and the more nervous specimens will usually respond well to gentle, consistent handling. It must be noted that some specimens will never tame down and I feel that it is cruel to stress such animals by forcing them to endure human contact against their will. Also, it is risky to try to assess the personality of a chondro at a reptile show. The stress of travel and exhibition often causes normally irritable animals to appear much more tame than they really are when acclimated and in a secure environment.

Myth # 2: "GTPs have enormous teeth."

While it is true that chondros do have impressive dentals, their teeth are nothing like the huge front fangs possessed by Emerald Tree Boas. A bite from an adult chondro will result in a series of tiny punctures from the incredibly sharp-tipped teeth, which may bleed freely for a few minutes. The majority of bites are inconsequential, and in my opinion hurt much less than getting stuck

Shed tooth from an adult *Morelia viridis*. All snakes regularly shed and replace teeth.

by briars. Nonetheless, bites are to be avoided, and with proper handling and feeding techniques, they should be rare. The greatest danger is sustaining a bite to the face and it is important to always protect yourself from exposing your face and eyes to a potential bite.

Myth # 3: "Wild GTPs eat a lot of birds."

Longer than average teeth and the arboreal habits of chondros have led to the speculation that birds make up an important food item in the diets of wild chondros. Field research does <u>not</u> support this, and the fecal matter of wild chondros does not seem to contain evidence of a lot of birds being eaten (Walsh, pers. com.). Certainly it is a safe assumption that a few birds are taken as prey, and it is likely that baby birds still in the nest may be the most frequent avian prey item. This may account for the fact that captive neonates can often be enticed into feeding on baby mice by scenting them with chick down. Caudal luring may entice birds in close enough to be seized, but there is a reason that the typical hunting posture of an adult chondro is head down . . . a posture much better suited to capturing small mammals as they pass by. The mental image of the tree-perched chondro snagging birds out of the air is likely erroneous.

Myth # 4: "You can tell the locality of a chondro by looking at it."

This is simply not true, even though it is one of the most widely accepted beliefs out there. The details about locality typing can be read in Chapter 3. *Some* chondros can be identified according to geographic race based on outward appearances, but this is not the same thing as making locality identification. With the extreme variability of chondro coloration and patterning, and the almost complete lack of verifiable collecting data available for founder stock, it is rather silly to believe that CB chondros can be sight-identified as belonging to a specific locality with anything approaching scientific accuracy.

Myth # 5: "If you treat a wild caught chondro for parasites, it is as good as buying a captive bred animal."

From a health standpoint, captive bred chondros are superior in every way to wild-collected animals. Wild-caught animals, even when treated for internal parasites, will never be the robust and vibrant animals that captive bred GTPs are. WC chondros seldom have the vigor, muscle tone, reproductive ability, tractable personalities, or lifespan that their CB counterparts have. They are far more susceptible to disease and stress-related issues. The money saved by buying cheap imports is more than offset by the potential veterinary bills and disappointments. Furthermore, you will be supporting an industry with a long history of unscrupulous dealers and inferior animals. Less than 50% of WC and farm-raised imports survive long in captivity.

Myth # 6: "GTPs are way too expensive."

Too expensive when compared to what? Chondro prices are set according to the free market principles of supply and demand. So are baseball cards. A Babe Ruth is worth a lot because of high demand and low supply. Quality chondros cost more to produce than non-established babies with no history or records, and aren't cranked out in huge numbers like colubrid snakes are. Many designer morphs are in especially high demand and low supply. It is amazing how many people expect breeders to sell their best stock for normal market prices, and make disparaging comments about greed and selfishness when breeders charge high prices for exceptional bloodlines, or hold back keepers for themselves. The fact is, CB chondros are expensive for valid reasons, just like other fine products offered to consumers. You don't buy a Mercedes for the price of a Chevy, and chondros are most definitely "the top of the line" when it comes to captive-produced reptiles. Personally, I will never buy a Mercedes because my value system will never allow me to spend that kind of money for a car. But, I will never go to a Mercedes dealer and whine that the cars should be priced like a Chevy, so I can afford one. Nor will I tell the Mercedes dealer that I'm tired of being told, "You get what you pay for!"

Myth # 7: "Chondros are difficult to keep, and are only for highly experienced keepers."

The truth is that chondros are more delicate to successfully keep than many other kinds of snakes, boids included. They have some specialized needs that must be understood and met for them to thrive, and they are not as tolerant of husbandry mistakes as are some other species. Because of this, some reptile keeping experience is highly recommended before acquiring your first chondro. Carpet Pythons make a good starter species. They are from the *Morelia* genus, but are hardier than chondros. Successfully keeping such less delicate kinds of snakes will help to develop the observational skills and instincts that are important to keeping chondros. All of this being said, GTPs are not difficult to maintain once their needs are understood and met, and will do very well for those who are willing to learn and listen. There will always be those whose skills and abilities are such that chondros are not the best choice for them. No truer words have been spoken than those commonly uttered by veteran keeper Trooper Walsh - "Chondros aren't for everybody." See Chapter 6 for much more on this subject.

Myth # 8: "GTPs need 100% humidity."

Chondros, being tropical in origin, need higher levels of humidity to do well and to shed properly than do many other kinds of snakes. There are frequent questions about how precise the relative humidity needs to be, and it is common for new keepers to believe that the animals require 100% humidity, and that cages must be kept dripping wet. In actuality, the animals will benefit from a cycle that includes a drying out period, and they can suffer health problems from living in a stagnant wet environment. Further, except during shedding cycles, the level of humidity is not critical as long as it is within acceptable parameters. This is covered in detail in Chapter 9.

Myth # 9: "GTPs are very prone to rectal prolapse."

It is true that anyone with a large collection of chondros will experience a prolapse sooner or later, and even the keeper of one animal may encounter this health problem. But to say that prolapse is a common occurrence with chondros, in the same way that regurgitation syndrome plagues Emerald Tree Boa keepers, is simply not true. Prolapse is usually very treatable, and in collections where the husbandry and cage environment is correctly administered and provided, *prolapse is not common*. The problem can occur even under the best conditions and to the most experienced keepers, however. Fear of this trouble should not be sufficient to keep anyone from working with the species. It is simply one more challenge to be dealt with as the need may arise. If potential for problems and challenges is not something you wish to deal with, then another kind of snake is recommended. For information about treating prolapse, see Appendix A.

Myth # 10: "GTPs should be fed only after they defecate."

With the exception of obviously constipated animals, you will underfeed and stunt the growth of your chondros if you follow this commonly given advice, which is mostly based on an unfounded fear of rectal prolapse. See Chapter 11 for the scoop (no pun intended) about feeding and defecation cycles.

Myth # 11: "Breeding two blue adults together will produce blue offspring."

You can substitute any color you like for "blue", but it won't make the statement any less incorrect. The fact is, chondro genetics are complicated, and adult colors are not the result of simple recessive, dominant, or co-dominant genes as they are in so many other reptiles. Your chances of getting offspring that will develop into adults with blue on them are higher when the parents have the trait, but what you are paying for with unchanged neonates is an *increased opportunity* for a blue adult. The better the past breeding results of specific adults, the better the chances are for getting desired results with current offspring. If chondro genetics were certain, the prices for some offspring would be much higher. Buying changed yearlings (at commensurately higher prices) is the way to go if knowing exactly what you are getting is very important to you. For most of us, watching the babies change and develop into a beautiful adult is a big part of what fascinates us about chondros.

Myth # 12: "Chondros are a sound financial investment."

Well, this depends on what is meant by investment. If your goal is to spend investment capital on something that will multiply rapidly for an early retirement, then chondros are *not* for you! Breeding chondros is incredibly challenging, and breeding them consistently is even more difficult. To really make a long-term profit, you will need to re-invest most or all of what you earn back into the enterprise. Caging and supplies, plus overhead, make up a substantial cost when setting up a breeding operation. There are always improvements to be made, and fresh stock to acquire. Starting the new hatchlings is something that must be experienced to be understood, and this difficulty alone weeds out many would-be breeders. Furthermore, a get-rich-quick mentality will never carry you through all that is needed to be a successful commercial chondro breeder... passion is needed for that.

However, if by "investment" you mean that you hope to be able to enjoy a hobby that has the real potential to pay for itself, or that you hope to enjoy some side income, then I would say that yes, chondros represent one of the best investments of money, time, and effort that a reptile keeper can make. Chondros are not only holding their own commercially but are increasing in value, which is very rare in the reptile business these days. The rewards of working with chondros are often are not measured financially, but can make you rich in personal achievement and satisfaction.

Section II. Captive Husbandry

Chapter 6. Are Chondros Right For You?

"The whole secret of a successful life is to find out what is one's destiny to do, and then to do it".

Henry Ford

A better way to phrase the title to this chapter would be, "Are you right for chondros?" Chondros are definitely not for everybody. While there are some who may take offense to this statement, no offense is intended. While it is my opinion that GTPs are not difficult to successfully keep and adequately care for, they do have special requirements that must be understood and met. That requires aptitude on the part of the would-be GTP owner, if the new snake is to thrive under his or her care. To make such a resolute statement as the one that opens this chapter is not a put-down; nor is it one of smug superiority: it is a fact that should be accepted. Every person has strengths and weaknesses, gifts and shortcomings; an important part of maturing as a person is learning those areas of personal strength, and exploiting them for good, as well as accepting that there are pursuits that don't fit well with our personal shortcomings. For example, I am at peace with the reality that I will never be a professional cyclist. I'm a big fan of Lance Armstrong, the American four-time Tour De France champion, and I enjoy riding racing bikes myself. Being a pro cyclist has made Lance very popular and financially well off, but I will never be one. I may have a burning desire for the money and prestige that pro cyclists have, and I may imagine myself trouncing my competitors as I climb the hills of Knox County, Ohio, but I will never excel in the sport of professional bike racing. Why? Because I do not possess the skills necessary to succeed. There are many skills required to be a successful pro cyclist, and I have almost none of them!

Likewise, there are some important skills needed to be a good chondro person. Some of them can be learned and developed, and some are inherent to specific personality types. Most are essential to initial success, and a few can be developed along the way. "Desire" is a good place to begin, but like my example of professional athletics, it is not nearly enough to simply "want" to keep chondros. I've known several individuals with a strong desire to work with chondros that came up short of success because they lacked one or more of the essential qualities needed. Along with the right skills, it is important to approach potential chondro ownership with the correct motives. We will discuss both issues in this chapter. It is hoped that the information will be a real help to those considering the purchase of a GTP, and will allow potential owners to "grade" themselves as to their personal capability as a keeper of these wonderful and challenging pythons. Judging from the frequency with which I am asked about this by those considering the species, the issue is an important one in which many people are interested.

Motives

There are many motivations for keeping and breeding chondros, or reptiles of any kind. Some are good and honorable, and some are not. The hobby of amateur herpetology has always attracted a wide range of personalities with many different motivations. Before the days when captive breeding, reptile shows, and the Internet began setting the pace, most amateur herp people were dedicated naturalists and field collectors. There were some odd fellows involved to be sure, but a lifelong fascination and love for reptiles and amphibians was the overwhelming motivation for the majority of herpers. Sadly, that has changed a lot in recent years, and far too many young hobbyists have had no exposure whatsoever to reptiles in the wild. Indeed, it is now mostly illegal to have anything to do with observing or collecting wild domestic reptiles or other herps in most states. Kauffeld's classic "Snakes and Snake Hunting", once a how-to primer for every budding herpetologist, is now an antiquated collection of stories from another era. While my friends and I spent our summers combing local fields, ponds, and marshes for whatever life we could find, newcomers to the hobby today are more inclined to have made their "discoveries" by pointing and clicking with a computer mouse. In my opinion, the passion for chondros is best experienced in the context of a love for all wildlife, and an appreciation for the grandeur and infinite beauty of nature. Let us ponder a few of the things that motivate people to keep chondros.

Prestige

There is no denying that a certain amount of prestige and status is often associated with the keeping and successful breeding of GTPs. I suppose that this is a part of owning any fine thing, whether it is a luxury car, an expensive musical instrument, a nice home, or whatever. People are funny; often the only requirement for possessing such things is a lot of money. While it may be natural to feel some pride in the ownership of expensive or desirable things, those who acquire such trophies out of some misplaced sense of personal exaltation are to be pitied. When a living animal becomes the means to accomplishing such a purpose, pity can turn to disgust. Chondros are not appropriate playthings for those in need of a status symbol.

Self Attention

Akin to those who seek status from the things they own are those who must always be at the center of attention, and use the allure and appeal of some thing to draw and keep the attention of others directed to themselves. Some snake keepers seem addicted to the public reaction they get when parading their animals openly. I was at an Independence Day parade a few years ago and spotted a man wearing a large constrictor around his neck along the crowded parade route. I confronted him about the danger, and the foolishness, of such an act. When he refused to contain the animal out of sight, I notified a local authority to deal with the man. This same immature need to use reptiles for individual egocentric agendas can be seen at many swap meets and on Internet forums.

Financial Gain

Those who begin building a collection of chondros with the goal of making a financial profit will almost certainly be disappointed. It takes a large operation, and the dedication of much time and energy to say nothing of the initial investment for livestock, cages, equipment, and facility to make more than a break-even income. It is true that chondros are one of the few reptile species that are maintaining and even increasing in value, but any financial rewards must be second to the fulfillment gained from simply working with these animals for the sheer enjoyment of experiencing them. I have often said, and truthfully so, that I would keep and breed chondros if they lost all commercial value. I admit that I would not be able to enjoy keeping them in the numbers I do if I were not able to make a living from them; but I would certainly have a nice collection, and work to produce some nice offspring. They are one of my life's passions, and were so for years before I made any money from selling them. Don't get into chondros because you think you will make a lot of quick money. The odds are against it, and you will eventually get frustrated and quit. I tell prospective breeders to plan on at least three to five years before seeing much success, and to assemble a group of at least a half-dozen animals.

Now that we have examined a few poor motives for keeping chondros, let's look at some good reasons to have them.

Passion

I feel that *passion* is the best motivation for working with any reptile species. Keepers that are the most passionate about the species they work with are usually the ones who make the breakthroughs; they are the ones who inspire passion in others; they are the ones who keep the focus on the animals and not themselves. Passion is what brings out the fullness of the enjoyment, the richness of the experience, and the depth of fulfillment. Passion is also the thing that makes you change the water bowls when you don't feel like it, get up in the wee hours of the morning to check the nest box, spend hours working with new hatchlings, and clean cages instead of going to the movies. Passion is what allows you to continue to be enthusiastic when there isn't much to be enthusiastic about. Life with chondros certainly has its high points and low points, but if passion is your primary motivation for having them, you will never go wrong. Passion is not preference; preference is simply choosing one over another. Passion is the thing that grips the heart and mind, and says, "I must do this!"

Challenge

Many of us need challenge in our lives, and a difficult goal is that much sweeter when it is finally obtained. While I don't consider the challenges of chondro keeping and breeding to be a proper motivation alone, there is no denying the appeal of stepping up to chondros from less exigent species. For me, the challenges of chondro keeping compliment and heighten my passion for them. When we undertake to conquer a challenge, we may fail before we succeed. Those who have a hard time experiencing disappointment, or tend to give up easily, or get quickly frustrated at the first sign of a problem, should probably seek an easier kind of snake to own. For those who patiently strive to overcome all obstacles, and desire to experience the kind of achievement that comes from stretching one's self to new levels, chondros can provide a unique and rewarding challenge.

Community

Few reptile species have inspired the kind of community that has developed around GTPs. Although I don't always prefer the company of people to animals, the friendships and relationships that I have made as a result of being a "chondrohead" are many, and valuable. Some of my closest friendships are those I made as a direct result of a mutual obsession with these green snakes. I have worked with many kinds of reptiles for most of my life and never have I experienced the kind of unity, camaraderie, and shared enthusiasm centered around a reptile such as is found in the worldwide chondro community. In July 2001, almost one hundred GTP aficionados from all over the U.S. and Canada converged on Maryland to participate in the first annual "ChondroFest". Hosted by Buddy Goetzger and Trooper Walsh, and dubbed the "Woodstock of Chondros" by those attending, ChondroFest provides a place for people of all backgrounds and levels of experience to enjoy sharing fellowship, food, and passion for GTPs. Many chondro people, like chondros themselves, are special.

Qualities of a Good Chondro Person

The following attributes are those I consider important, even essential, to the successful keeping of GTPs. These qualities are also important if you are seriously interested in breeding the species. The list is intended to be a guide to the important qualities you will need, and the better you are at developing them, the higher your chances of success with chondros, and probably many other areas of life as well. Chondros can teach all of us a lot about ourselves.

Experienced

The amount, and quality, of your experience with keeping and breeding herps will directly impact your success with chondros. A frequent question asked by those considering moving into the keeping of arboreals is, "How much experience do I need?" The answer is relative, and difficult to phrase in terms of exact measures, but in general I would recommend several years of successfully keeping a variety of reptiles, snakes in particular. Three years would be a good minimum to start out with, and if you have worked with something a bit more demanding than entry level colubrids like Cornsnakes or California Kingsnakes, so much the better. It has been observed by several keepers that perhaps the best "trainer" species for working up to chondros is the Carpet Python (*Morelia spilota*). These pythons are hardier than their green relatives, but share some common habits and needs. Being more tolerant of husbandry errors, and a lot less expensive, they are an attractive and effective bridge to chondro keeping.

Why is experience necessary? Largely because experience develops other qualities that you will need, that are detailed below. There are many things an experienced keeper just "knows", things that are difficult to put in writing and that may even be subconsciously understood, but make up an important part of daily husbandry. A general familiarity with captive reptiles - how they act when they are happy and content, how they look when something is not quite right - will be of enormous advantage when learning to care for chondros. Any trouble that you may have encountered and problems you have solved while working with less demanding species, will be helpful in building your confidence and troubleshooting abilities.

It should be noted that simply having a long life list of reptile species under one's belt is not necessarily the same thing as having good experience. By the time I was seventeen, I had kept a huge number of different herps from many taxa. But this did not mean I was ready for chondros, because much of my early years were spent with my collection in a state of flux, and as a result I did not develop much of a familiarity or level of expertise with any one group. I am frequently contacted by young enthusiasts, asking me if they are ready to keep GTPs, and invariably they say, "I have a cornsnake, an iguana, and a Boa constrictor". I always encourage such young people, for they are the future of our hobby and deserve to have their enthusiasm watered, not squelched. But chondros are a species that will do best under the care of those who have a bit more hands-on training than a brief career with common snakes.

Teachable

Willingness to learn and to be corrected is extremely important to becoming a knowledgeable and experienced chondro keeper. I am called on to give advice on virtually a daily basis, often spending several hours a day answering e-mail and forum questions, and I am always encountering those folks who want to do things their own way and are simply looking for my endorsement. When I tell keepers to house chondros individually, or to feed dead prey, or to provide a horizontal thermal cage gradient, or to avoid buying chondros from general reptile dealers, I am trying to get them in a position to experience the best chances for success. So much of the time, when they do the opposite of what I suggest to them, I wonder why they bothered to ask! Others and myself invest an enormous amount of time in helping inexperienced keepers extricate themselves from problems that are easily avoidable, and it is often very apparent that some individuals have a problem listening. I spend far more time helping these people than I do my own customers, so I know what I'm talking about! A friend of mine, also a knowledgeable keeper, recently estimated that about 50% of the advice he gives out is ignored, with predictable consequences.

Chondros are not like most other snakes, and they pose unique challenges to even experienced keepers. The time to experiment and deviate from established and proven techniques is after you have some years of chondro experience, and have gained a deep familiarity with the needs and habits of these animals. Chondro husbandry is best approached with an open mind and a willingness to set aside preconceived ideas and personal tastes, or a need to prove you can do things your own way; be willing to listen and learn from those who have already been through the learning curve. With the abundance of good information available these days, there is no need to make major errors, yet every week new chondro enthusiasts make the same mistakes and encounter the same pitfalls.

Those contemplating becoming chondro keepers should spend considerable time researching all they can find about caging, husbandry, and other related issues, and should begin building relationships with experienced keepers and breeders. One of the very best ways to introduce yourself to chondros and chondro keeping is to visit an experienced person, spending some hours observing, asking questions, and learning. Often there are several effective ways to approach a technique or problem, and you will gain a good understanding of the principles of basic GTP care by seeing how successful keepers do things. Make sure the person instructing you knows what they are talking about and has proven experience with the kind of results you would like to have yourself.

Observant

If you are the kind of person who is not given to making intelligent and analytical observations about your world, then chondros may not be the best choice for you. This does not mean that those not keeping chondros are stupid or dull! Rather, I'm simply recognizing that some people are observant and some are not. Things that leap out to one person are completely ignored by another. "Didn't you notice this?" is a question I frequently want to ask when aiding a troubled keeper. Good keepers notice everything, and don't tend to blow off small details, but take pains to document and follow daily events and changes for possible importance. Good keepers also make frequent checks of their animals, as time allows. It is difficult to imagine a responsible chondro keeper who, having been absent for the better part of a day, doesn't make a prompt check of the chondros upon his or her return.

Detail-Oriented

I admit it - I am a compulsive, obsessive person - and a prime candidate for both stress management counseling, and chondro keeping! Seriously, GTPs are not good animals to keep if you tend to be sloppy, cluttered, and carefree. Good chondro keepers don't need to be told that water bowls need to be scrubbed rather than simply refilled…they already do that out of habit. They change the substrate in tubs when it becomes stale, whether it has been soiled or not. An attention to detail, and the development of good habits, is a part of the makeup of excellent keepers, and it shows in their collections and breeding results. This doesn't mean that only neurotic individuals and fanatics can successfully work with chondros… but it helps! At a minimum, successful keepers must be willing to pay strict attention to proper hygiene and to develop good and consistent care habits and routines.

Instinctual

The dictionary defines instinct as "the innate aspect of behavior that is unlearned; a natural aptitude". In everyday terms, this means that a person with good instincts can assess a situation, and without being told, make a basic judgment of the situation and take some action which is more correct than incorrect. On the basketball court, I have no instincts other than bad ones. I will do the wrong thing almost every time. My peers learned this fact early in my academic career, and it resulted in my always being chosen last for basketball! But put me on a lake with a bass rod, and chances are we'll not go hungry, because I have good instincts about where to find bass. In the same way, there are some people who just don't have good instincts with chondros. This may sound elitist but it is the truth just the same. I have seen chondros that were nearly dead from horrible care and decisions made by the owner, which were quickly salvaged and restored to health by someone who knew what they were doing. Such owners lack much more than simple know-how; they have no basic instincts for the care and nurturing of such a delicate animal as a chondro. Some instincts can be developed along the way, and nobody starts out as an expert, but those wishing to enjoy healthy and thriving GTPs must possess good instincts for the task. This is perhaps the most important attribute I look for when helping new keepers. Some refer to this as having "Chondro Zen", but whatever name you put on it, it needs to be present in some degree.

Patient

People tell me all the time that I am patient. I do not think this is so. To me, patience implies a rare kind of saintliness that genuinely embraces hardship, and smiles through trials and adversity. This is not me! What I do have is endurance, which I define as an ability to stick it out to the end and never give up or quit until the objective is reached. Most people think this is patience, so that's what we'll call it. But, regardless of the word used, a chondro keeper must possess some of it. Chondros are prone to frustrate us with a wide variety of behaviors, carefully calculated to push us over the edge. Males (and sometimes females) go off feed; animals of both sexes can act constipated, experience bad sheds under ideal humidity, lie on the floor, and undergo personality changes. If you desire to breed these snakes, you had better quadruple your level of patience, because you have never experienced anything like starting up a dozen or so little worms that refuse to eat anything you offer them.

This is an age of instant gratification. We microwave our frozen food, get cash out of a box in the wall at the bank, send instant messages electronically around the world, and flip through two hundred channels without moving more than our thumb. Chondros are a reality check in this fast-paced, high-tech world. They live in their own time zone, at their own pace. They mature slowly, and gradually become parents…maybe. You don't power feed chondros and crank out babies from young, accelerated females, and when males go off feed, they resume eating when they are ready… not when you are. They are not a hurry-up-and-do-it kind of animal. I have been privileged to spend some time in the tropics, in so-called "third-world" countries, and one thing you notice right away is that life is much slower in these places. There is time to breathe, to hear, and to slow down and to listen. Chondros seem to bring that kind of relaxation and peace into my life, and they have not forgotten the slower pace of the quiet rain forests from whence they came. You are not going to change them… but you can allow them to change you.

Able to devote sufficient funds

This last keeper characteristic can sometimes be a bone of contention with those who seem to think that they are owed anything they want, especially some members of the younger generation. Chondros are not inexpensive, and for good reasons. Even entry-level animals, if captive bred and well-started, are outside of the means of most teenage incomes. Besides the cost of the animal itself, there is the matter of a proper cage. This should be based on what the animal needs to thrive, not what you happen to have on hand. You will also need a heater, thermostat, light, and basic cage accouterments. You will also need a good thermometer, spray bottle, hook, feeding tongs, and disinfectant. It is often common to have as much money invested in equipment as in the chondro, and if a person can't or won't make this investment, then it is the wrong time for the acquisition of a species that requires a considerable outlay of cash. Many people, young people especially, want what they want *now* and often will skimp on caging and equipment, trying to cut corners while providing the animal a home.

Chondro owners should also be in a financial position to get veterinary care for their animals if and when they need it. Even healthy chondros can suffer a prolapse or a respiratory infection that requires professional treatment, and a routine visit and the medication needed can run a couple hundred dollars. If you can't afford that, then you have a responsibility to refrain from taking an animal into your care for which you may not be able to get adequate medical attention.

This does not mean that chondros are only for the wealthy - I am not wealthy. Most of us can find a way to afford what we want, and in the U.S. there are wide-open opportunities to earn what you are worth, and to become worth more if you choose. Often, the financial rewards that result from hard work and time spent paying your dues aren't realized until adulthood. It is best, and well worth your while, to become established financially before making a commitment to work with chondros. The hobby is much more enjoyable, and the animals' needs better accommodated, when the keeper can afford to spend what is required to do things correctly. It can be offensive to be repeatedly asked, as most breeders are, to sell our beautiful and carefully produced offspring for half of what they are worth, because "that is all I have to spend". How many people would walk into a Mercedes dealership, and demand half price because that is all they have in their checkbook?

Are you ready?

This chapter may seem to be overly negative in tone to you. I hope this is not the case, but if so, I can only say that everything I have written here has come from the direct experience of years of serving keepers of all levels. This is the one chapter of this book that may have been written more for those who should not have chondros than for those who do, and some of them (as I am all too familiar with) do not like to be told what they need to hear. Many people seem destined to learn many things the hard way; I have endeavored to honestly and clearly spell out what you should expect of yourself to have success with GTPs. It is sincerely hoped that the information in this chapter will turn more people into candidates for chondrohood, than it will turn away. Anybody who is willing to listen and learn, and has basic skills with reptile husbandry, can be a successful chondro person. Are you such a person? In the next chapter we will discuss what you need to know to get started with a quality, healthy animal. Good luck!

Chapter 7. How to Buy a Quality Chondro

"It's unwise to pay too much, but it's worse to pay too little. When you pay too much, you lose a little money...that is all. But when you pay too little you sometimes lose everything, because the thing you bought was incapable of being the thing it was bought to be. The Common Law of business balance prohibits paying a little and getting a lot, it can't be done. If you deal with the lowest bidder, it is well to add something for the risk you run and if you do that you will have enough to pay for something better."

John Ruskin

Absolutely the most important ingredient to happiness and success with your new chondro, besides your own responsibilities, is obtaining the right animal for you. Making a wise choice will usually mean long-term satisfaction and help when you need it; choosing poorly almost always results in frustration, disappointment, and little or no follow-up service. It is imperative that the most important choice you will make - whom to buy from - is made with a full knowledge of the facts, and is based on a firm relationship of trust.

Quality

First, let's define "quality" in the context of this discussion. A quality chondro is any ***captive bred, honestly represented, healthy animal*** that can be reasonably expected to thrive when given proper care by the new owner. It may be from the most exotic designer bloodline and cost many thousands of dollars, or it may be a plain green animal from the first clutch of a proud new breeder. Quality does not imply that animals from "big name" breeders are better than those from someone few have heard of, or that very costly animals are superior to less expensive ones, as long as the animals are all are healthy and honestly represented. Some bloodlines are more attractive than others in terms of color and history, but any healthy captive bred chondro, backed up with service after the sale and having hatch and feeding data, is a quality one.

Buy Captive Bred

The one thing that must be firmly established at the outset is to buy only domestic captive bred chondros. Let me repeat this, because failure to do so is the single greatest cause of problems for new owners: Buy *only* documented, domestically captive bred animals. The importance of this cannot be over emphasized. Captive bred chondros are superior in every way to imported or "farm-raised" animals. They are more robust, are better able to resist diseases and stress-related difficulties and they are generally free of parasites and blemishes, both of which are common with imports. They have better muscle tone, greater longevity, make better breeders, and acclimate more readily to captivity. There is no valid reason for most chondro buyers to even consider buying anything other than a captive bred animal. Buying an inferior, inexpensive chondro in the hope of "making it work" is about as wise as the girl who marries an alcoholic, believing her love will save him… the odds in both cases are against success. Commit to buying CB chondros only, and learn how to spot and avoid imposters. Equally important, make sure any CB baby you buy has been well-established, or you will probably be disappointed… more on this shortly.

Imports do have a small, legitimate role in the chondro market. Experienced breeders may wish to work with imports for a number of reasons, including the opportunity to acquire wild blood or to obtain animals that are not available from captive bred bloodlines, such as pure specimens of geographic races. However, the majority of imported animals in the U.S. are sold for no such purposes; they are sold to unsuspecting customers who often buy them as impulse purchases at swap meets or from Internet classifieds. Most of these animals are priced far below the normal market value, and appeal to those who don't realize that with chondros, you absolutely get what you pay for, and you don't get what you don't pay for. A few vendors, realizing that an educated buying public is beginning to get that message, are hiking their prices to the level of captive bred stock in an apparent effort to add credibility to the animals.

Selecting a Source

Almost as important as buying captive bred is who you decide to buy from. Again, the rule to follow to stay out of trouble is to only buy from a reputable breeder. Such a breeder is dedicated to his animals and to your success. He or she can provide you with a well-started, established animal with a background history, and can answer your questions and help you get off to a great start. More importantly, a reputable breeder will stand behind the sale and will be there for you if there is a problem. It is truly amazing how many new GTP owners require help each year with non-feeding babies or other beginner trouble, but don't hold the seller of the animal to any standard of accountability.

Swap Meets and Expos

Avoid buying any chondro from a swap meet or expo vendor, *unless* you have a relationship with them that includes references. While there are some legitimate reptile show vendors selling good quality animals, there are also large numbers of them who will look you in the eye and tell you anything you want to hear. I made my living for several years selling reptile cages with my company, CageMaster, at reptile shows and expos and I do know what I am talking about! Even "breeders" expos are often full of imports and misrepresented animals. I know of two different reptile dealers that were temporarily banned from participating in a "breeders" expo for selling imported chondros. At one of these events, which clearly prohibits imports of any kind, I asked a dealer who was displaying what were obviously imported, yearling-aged Biaks at his table, "Who produced these animals?" "I don't know", he told me. "We just got them in last night." Not only is this practice deceptive to the buyers, it is a slap in the face to any of the legitimate breeders in attendance who worked hard to produce and establish healthy captive bred stock. A chondro is a bad item to purchase on impulse, or from some guy at a show table who is trained to sell, sell, sell. Most inexperienced buyers are not qualified to discern an import from a captive bred animal. Many of these vendors have dozens of chondros on the table along with large quantities of other herps. Quite frankly, it isn't possible for these individuals to have produced the numbers of chondros they claim are captive bred. Even large-scale private breeders usually have waiting lists, and seldom have dozens of animals of all different ages setting around. Such venues are a poor choice for a place to shop for a new chondro. If you do buy from a show vendor, make sure you know with whom you are dealing.

Shows and expos can be a good place to meet breeders and form relationships for doing business in the future.

Internet Classifieds

Also to be avoided are Internet classifieds. Some of the larger classified sites are chock full of highly questionable animals, some so bad they become the brunt of jokes on other boards. Like the swap meets, there are some legitimate animals offered from time to time, but the novice is not qualified to sort them out. Even on the Chondroweb Classifieds, where experienced breeders screen the ads, and strict rules govern what may be advertised, it is "buyer beware". As always, *know who you are buying from*, and avoid giving in to the temptation to buy from an unknown source. Price should be one of the last considerations when looking for a breeder, not the first one. You get what you pay for, and recently, many less-than-reputable vendors have shifted to selling online via classified boards. In some ways, buying this way is even more risky than buying at a show table, because you are buying sight-unseen with nothing but the seller's word to go on, and possibly some distorted, color-enhanced digital images.

Dedicated Breeders

The very best source for your first chondro is a well-known, reputable breeder that can give you references from satisfied customers. There are such breeders, some big and some small, but all dedicated to your success. It is best to establish a relationship with several breeders when first looking into buying a chondro, and find the one you are most comfortable with. Ask a lot of questions and avoid breeders who don't seem interested in helping you. Find out what guarantees, if any, the breeder may offer about the health of the animal. While most breeders, myself included, expect you to understand that sales of live animals are final, a reputable breeder will stand behind his animals and will do what he or she can to help you with any problems that may arise. You should expect nothing less than excellent service after the sale, so discuss this with the breeder, and take your business elsewhere if you aren't comfortable with the attitude or answers you receive. The better breeders will supply you with feeding and shedding records, and hatch data that includes hatch date, hatch weight, and sire and dam information. A few breeders will even have a bloodline pedigree, showing your animal's bloodline history going back to the wild founder stock. The breeder should be willing to show you his or her collection, the parents of your animal, and discuss with you any questions or problems you may have about your setup. With resources such as the better shows and expos, ChondroWeb and the ChondroForums, and other online sites, it is not difficult to meet and get to know some of the best breeders around. See Appendix B for a partial list to get you started.

Most breeders producing selectively bred chondros are quite popular, and need to keep waiting lists, or "first-refusal" lists, for upcoming hatches. Producing true captive bred, established babies is a time-consuming

The most important thing a prospective chondro buyer should do is to establish a relationship with a dedicated breeder. Here, the author (on the right) discusses the purchase of a yearling with a new GTP enthusiast.

process, and both the breeder and the buyer will need to exercise some of that patience we talked about in the last chapter. Sometimes you will be fortunate, and there will be some good animals available when you first begin looking, but more often you will probably have to wait. Use this period to establish a relationship with the breeder, and if possible, make a visit and see the facility and animals in person. Many breeders respect this show of desire and commitment on your part, and will respond accordingly.

Selecting Your First Chondro

For your very first chondro, you would be wise to consider a slightly older animal over a hatchling. While little baby chondros are without a doubt one of the most appealing creatures around, and the anticipation of watching yours grow and go through its color change may be strong, you will be safer cutting your teeth on a yearling, or at least an older baby six to eight months old. Such an animal will be very well-established, its immune system will be more developed, and it will be out of the more delicate baby stage. This also means it will tolerate slight handling errors better, errors which might damage a fragile hatchling, causing spinal

117

damage that often shows up later. Buying a yearling also means you will have a much better idea of how it will look as an adult, and it may possibly be sexed as well. *Never* buy a sexed hatchling under a year in age! See the comments below.

If you do decide to buy a young hatchling, make sure that it is very well-established. This means that the animal will be at least three months old, will have shed twice, and will have eaten on its own at least ten to twelve times. Ads that represent babies as having "eaten three times" may be true, but three meals is nothing when it comes to establishing baby chondros. Most need at least ten meals before they are really feeding aggressively. There are exceptions to this, and some babies will eat aggressively right out of the egg, or after a few meals. It is important to establish a trust relationship with the seller, because you can't tell until it is too late that you have been sold a non-feeder. Even babies that have voluntarily eaten a few meals may go off feed from the stress of being moved or shipped, and will need to be started again, virtually from scratch. It is therefore extremely important that you buy an established baby that has put on some growth.

When picking out your baby or yearling, look for an animal that appears filled-out and with good weight. Avoid a thin animal with the ribs accentuated, a bony spinal ridge, or any skin wrinkles, other than normal folds of skin where the body bends. Be especially wary of any horizontal folds in the skin, as these can indicate dehydration or malnutrition. The animal should look sleek and glossy, with good muscle tone, not dry looking or flaccid. Avoid animals that have dried pieces of shed stuck on them. While this is easily remedied and is not in and of itself a health threat, it may indicate the animal has been kept too dry and may suffer dehydration problems or kidney stress. Likewise, avoid puffy or bloated animals that appear to be full of fluid, as this usually indicates kidney problems. If the animal is large enough to be safely handled, ask to hold it. Let it slide through your hands, and feel the dorsal area with your thumb as it moves, checking for any kinks, lumps, or indentations. Babies should not be handled this way, but can be visually inspected as they crawl. Look at the eyes, nose, mouth, and labial pits, and make sure they are free of matter. Ensure the tongue flicks normally, and that the animal moves with confidence, and has no hint of neurological disorders which may cause it to quiver or hold itself in an odd way. The time to discover a problem is now, not after you have had the animal a few days. Chondros are fragile creatures as babies, and they can have small defects that not even the breeder has noticed, so inspect your potential purchase carefully.

Chondros have many different personality types, just like people, and you may not be able to tell much about yours from interacting with it during the daylight hours. Ask the breeder to lightly prod the animal. Most younger chondros will become agitated and snappy when pestered this way, and this will show you how alert the animal is. Listen carefully as it breathes heavily; respiratory infections can often be heard as wheezing. Note: Some babies make a little clicking or popping sound when disturbed, but this is normal. Not all chondros will react when prodded, and some will bury the head in their coils. This is especially true of yearling and older animals, and is also normal. Most snappy babies will begin to calm down on their own as they mature, usually beginning at around twelve to eighteen months of age, and snappy babies are often good feeders, so don't be alarmed about buying a baby with an aggressive personality. You should not be handling babies under a year in age anyway, until you gain some experience.

The parents of your chondro, and to a lesser extent the other animals in the family tree, will largely determine the potential adult colors. Choosing a healthy animal, and a reputable and honest breeder, are much more important than the potential colors of the animal when it comes to selecting your first chondro. Forget about any "locality" claims when looking for your first chondro. Maroon and yellow babies alike can make attractive adults, and there is no difference in temperament, gender, or any other important factor between them. You will probably pay more for a dark baby, and yearlings generally cost more than hatchlings as well. For those interested in my thoughts about grading babies for potential adult colors, see Chapter 15.

If you are buying an animal over the Internet without seeing it first, make sure you know and trust the breeder. It makes sense in this age of mass communication and air shipping capabilities that honest and legitimate transactions will take place between people who live far away from each other, possibly in different countries or even continents. Again, a trust relationship is the foundation for a wise purchase when acquiring animals this way. For a first chondro, it is strongly suggested to buy from a breeder close enough to visit and to get to know.

Neonate Sexing

Here is another rule for new buyers: Never, never buy a sexed chondro that is less than a year in age. This is because the fragile spines and vertebrae of baby chondros are not developed or strong enough to safely withstand the technique of probing the tail to determine the sex of the animal. Even worse is the practice of "popping" the animal to determine sex. This involves the forcing out of the hemipenes of males with thumb pressure. This is a common and safe practice with hatchling colubrids and some boids, but should never be done to chondros of any age. I need to emphasize that no reputable breeder these days sexes baby chondros, because of the risk of damage to the baby. Such sexed offspring may develop spinal kinks as they mature, kinks that used to be assumed to be genetic flaws but are now known to be the result of damage from sexing. Even if most of the babies sexed by a dealer are not damaged, the practice is cruel to the few that are. Do you want to risk being the customer who ends up with a kinked animal, even if some other sexed babies are undamaged? Understand that damage from sexing chondros too young often does not show up until later. I have seen kinked animals in private collections that came from dealers who insist that "they are experienced enough to do it right". Don't do it! Waiting until chondros are a year or so in age before sexing them is something that responsible keepers and breeders (and buyers) understand and accept. Unless you are buying an animal specifically for breeding, gender is not important, and if you simply must know the sex of your animal before buying, stick to yearlings or young adults.

Supporting Captive Breeding

When you spend your hard earned dollars on any product or service, you are voting with your checkbook. The restaurants we choose to eat at, the businesses we buy our gasoline, our clothes, and our groceries from; the make of automobile we drive and the dealership we buy it from; all these decisions serve to sustain a business model and level of service we prefer, while contributing to the decrease and possible failure of others. In the same way, we make a critical judgment when we spend money on our hobbies and leisure pursuits. Dedicated breeders are responsible for the incredible wealth of heritage, information, and wide assortment of exceptional and healthy chondros available today. Without them, chondros would mostly be regarded as an exotic and misunderstood species that few could or would work with, and the heavy losses and failure rates of years gone by would still be the norm. Breeders have established a genetically diverse, thriving population of chondros worldwide, have developed and published the techniques and methods that have allowed many others to enjoy the same success with both long term husbandry and breeding, and have funded and developed the beautiful color and pattern morphs we all thrill to. Contrast these achievements with the cruel treatment many imported animals suffer, the hundreds of frustrated and disappointed first time owners who have failed to get their animal to thrive and have possibly even quit the hobby, and the misinformation and deception practiced by animal dealers in direct competition with those of us who have worked so hard to raise chondro keeping to the level it has achieved. Which of these two groups deserve to be supported and perpetuated by you? And which group do you wish to be a part of?

Chapter 8. Proper Caging

"Efficiency is concerned with doing things right. Effectiveness is doing the right things."

                Peter F. Drucker

I have remarked at times, only half facetiously, that I could keep a chondro healthy in a five gallon plastic bucket if I had to. Don't misunderstand me, I certainly am not recommending anybody try that! My point is this - if the fundamental requirements for housing chondros are understood, then meeting them is not difficult, and there are many ways of accomplishing this important goal. As a reptile cage expert, I can categorically state that there is no perfect reptile cage. I have been building snake cages since I was about eight years old, and I have made them using every conceivable material and incorporating all the design factors you could think of. I founded the very successful cage manufacturing and distributing company, CageMaster, and I know what I am talking about when it comes to cages for chondros.

CageMaster "Chondro Condos" from 1994 still in use by the author as cycling and breeding cages.

CageMaster even marketed a unit specifically for arboreals, and at the time of writing I have some of those original "Chondro Condos" still in everyday use. In fact, I have produced every clutch in my history as a chondro breeder in these units. However, learning and technology marches on, and today there are even better designs and equipment. In this chapter I will give in-depth analysis of the range of cage materials, designs, and some of the commercial cages available, as well as a description of the cages I make and use myself these days. The first part of this chapter provides information specifically about caging for adult GTPs. Housing for yearlings and neonates will be covered in the latter part of the chapter.

Cage Materials

There are many materials used to make chondro cages, both by those making their own cages as well as commercially manufactured units. There are advantages and disadvantages to most, and a few that are just not well-suited to the moist environment chondros need. The most important qualities for chondro cage materials are an ability to hold in heat, and to hold up in a humid environment without deteriorating. I'll begin with the least suited materials, and work toward the best.

Screen

There are cages available that are basically a frame of some kind, covered on all sides with screen. Most of these are designed and intended for lizards. Unless you live in a humid, tropical location, such cages are nearly worthless as chondro environments, because the screen construction makes it impossible to maintain a heated and humid interior. Also, there is the danger of your chondros rubbing their noses raw on all that screen, especially males during breeding periods when they can be quite active.

Glass

Once upon a time, glass aquariums were the only thing snake keepers had available commercially to house their animals, and some keepers today still use them for chondros. To be sure, an aquarium can be made to work, and they are used successfully by a number of keepers and at least a couple successful breeders. However, they have some distinct disadvantages, and are not the best choice, especially for beginners. Unfortunately, because they are cheap and readily available, beginners are most likely to use them, but cost should never be the primary consideration when choosing chondro caging. However, the low price, availability, and clear view they provide of the occupants, all combine to make aquariums an attractive choice to some.

One problem with using glass to house chondros is that it has a relatively low R-value, which makes it a poor choice for holding heat. The construction industry assigns an R-value to different kinds of materials so that consumers can understand the insulation properties of each material. A higher R-value means the material will allow the transfer, or loss, of heat more slowly than materials with a lower R-value, such as glass. Another major disadvantage of aquariums is the fact that they are top opening, and a suitable lid and top must be purchased or constructed that will allow some ventilation, but not excessive heat and humidity loss. When this top is opened or removed, there will be a lot of heat loss no matter how well the design works otherwise. Working out the balance between ventilation, and heat and humidity loss, along with the skills needed to construct a top, make aquariums a less than ideal choice for many. Aquariums are also prone to breakage, can't be stacked because of top access, and can't be drilled for installation of heaters, perches, etc. I also feel that chondros are more secure when not exposed on all sides. Some like them, but I think aquariums are best suited for what they were designed for… fish.

Acrylic

In recent years, cages made of acrylic have become somewhat popular, and were brought to the attention of the public by Tony Nicoli, a collector that had a number of these cages made for housing his Emerald Tree Boas and chondros. This is the only type of cage material discussed here that I have not had any hands-on experience with, so my comments are theoretical. Being thicker than many kinds of plastic, acrylic cages probably hold heat fairly well. The cages certainly are impressive visually, and make an artistic display. Since acrylic can be drilled and cut, these cages are more functional than aquariums because ventilation and access doors can be incorporated into the sides while allowing a solid top. Three things would concern me about these cages, providing the heat and humidity issues were not a problem. These are: Lack of security for the animals from being exposed on all sides; the scratching of the acrylic from cleaning; and the problem of water spotting and streaking from misting. I would personally tire quickly of the very modern "artsy" look of these cages, but this is purely due to my own tastes. There are breeders who use and like this type of cage.

Wood

Wood has several advantages that make it a popular consideration for those making their own cages, and for home-based small commercial operations. Wood is readily available in a variety of natural and manufactured products, has a relatively high R-value so it holds heat well, and is relatively inexpensive. It can be worked with using common home workshop power tools. All of these qualities make it the material of choice for many cage builders.

The biggest disadvantage of wood and wood byproducts is that they are porous, which means they absorb moisture and odors, and will be damaged by the stains and degradation that accompany them. Even wood materials rated for exterior use must be sealed or covered, and will be ruined if continually exposed to moisture. Laminating the wood with some kind of impervious covering solves this problem, but this can be time consuming and/or expensive. Using a commercial laminate such as Formica works very well, and usually this type of surface will stand up to years of moisture and scrubbing. After all, this is more than likely what your kitchen counter tops are covered with. These laminates must be installed with contact cement and trimmed before any of your cage panels are assembled, and require skill and the proper tools for a good job. Because of these considerations, most weekend cage builders opt for painting or sealing wood with a film finish such as polyurethane. These film finishes consist of solids suspended in a carrying agent that evaporates after you apply it, leaving the solids to form a semi-protective film if enough coatings are applied. Notice I said "semi" because all film finishes eventually degrade and must be reapplied. The fumes from the evaporating carrying agent can be dangerous to you and your animals until completely cured, which can take days. Because of all these factors, I consider wood a poor choice for a humid cage, unless the builder is able to apply an appropriate laminate.

Melamine

Melamine is a laminated wood byproduct, and would seem to be a good material for use in chondro cages. I have made many hundreds of cages and tub racks out of melamine, including some chondro cages which are still in use at my facility and have seen over seven years of daily use. And while I can honestly say that there are worse materials to use than melamine, it is not an ideal board to use for wet environments. The laminated surface of melamine is the same stuff that commercial countertop laminate is made from, but it is much thinner. The thickness and quality of this laminate is what determines how well a particular brand will hold up, and not all melamine is created equal. The stuff you can buy from home improvement stores is normally not the best grade, and some kinds are even laminated with a paper face. These kinds of melamine will degrade quickly when subjected to moisture, and even the best grades and brands will eventually show discoloration, surface dimpling, or swelling. With reasonable care, proper sealing of corner seams, and using a high quality board, you can expect to get several years of service out of your melamine cages, but my idea of an ideal material is one that does not have a built-in failure rate after a certain length of time. Melamine cages hold heat very well, but are quite heavy. An expensive specialty saw blade is needed to cut melamine without it chipping badly.

Plastic

As a material, plastic has one huge advantage over wood for use in a wet environment - it is waterproof. Because of this fact alone many keepers will use nothing else, and I can see their reasoning. However, not all plastics and plastic cages are ideal. And, most home cage builders

Vision cages are one popular brand of plastic cage for arboreals and can be modified to meet the needs of chondros. This one has been equipped with a heat panel, thermostat, silk plants, natural wood perches, and a fluorescent light.

do not have the tools and skills to make their own plastic cages.

The biggest downside to using plastics for chondro cages is that many have a low R-value and allow too much heat loss. If you have trouble keeping a cage warm, then it really doesn't matter how waterproof it is. Some plastic cages need the entire room to be kept to a certain level of warmth or they just will not hold heat well, and this can make it more difficult to establish a thermal gradient in the cage. Furthermore, some plastic cages are prone to cracking over time, while others will melt if exposed to heat lamps. Most commercially available plastic cages are too open in construction, requiring owner modification to get them to hold humidity well. Some also have built-in lips and ridges where snakes can hang, hide, and defecate, making husbandry more difficult than it needs to be. Some plastic cages are designed in a way that prevents stacking. Many plastic cages lose heat rapidly and re-heat slowly, making them a poor choice when cycling for breeding. All of these problems can be a lot to trade off, just to get a waterproof surface.

Happily, there is a company that has solved much of the shortcomings of plastic cages …Habitat Systems. HS uses a double-walled, hollow

A Habitat Systems cage with built-in heat panel, fluorescent light, and synthetic wood perches. Mulch and silk plants add to the function and appearance of the cage. Condensation from humidity is visible on the inside of the open door.

plastic panel that is thermally efficient. Ventilation is not excessive, and the cages hold humidity well. They are available with lights, heat panels, and synthetic wood perches installed, ready to use except for a thermostat. In my opinion, they are as close to an ideal commercial chondro cage as is currently available. Add some silk jungle plants to dress up the rather Spartan white interior, and you will have a very serviceable cage that will last for years. These cages (and most plastic cages, in my opinion) have visual shortcomings and are not the most attractive way to go, but much of this can be overcome with tasteful cage décor. For those concerned only with function, HS cages are an excellent choice. HS cages are not inexpensive, but to repeat: Cost should not be the prime consideration when choosing chondro caging. It should be noted that several popular brands of plastic cages are successfully used by keepers, shortcomings not withstanding.

My Cages

Those of you who are familiar with my web site are already aware of my cage designs, and that I have complete plans for building them published

One wall of the author's main chondro room showing his custom home-made cages.

A corner area of the author's main room showing custom corner units. One big benefit to custom caging is the ability to have special sized and shaped units that maximize the use of a small space.

there. As mentioned at the beginning of this chapter, there is no perfect chondro cage, but the cages I make and use myself come as close, for my taste and purposes, as I have found. Making your own cages can save a lot of money if you have access to the right tools, and you also can tailor the specs to your exact needs.

I have combined the benefits of wood with an easy, safe, and inexpensive way of waterproofing, and that is to cover all the interior cage surfaces with waterproof contact paper. I use Contac® paper in Hunter Green, but any paper will work so long as it is totally waterproof. Contac® paper is actually thin plastic that stretches rather than tears when pulled. If you have any doubts about a particular brand, use some to line the interior of a bowl or tub, and let it set overnight full of water. If the paper holds the water without discoloring or softening, then it should work for you. The paper I use is pretty tough, resisting abrasions and holding up well to mild wiping. If it is accidentally cut or abraded, a small patch can be cut and applied over the area and is almost invisible. Waterproof seams can be made by overlapping the joints an inch or two. I have also come to prefer the dark green interior of these cages to the white interior of melamine or plastic cages, and I feel the animals are more secure. Building my own cages gives me complete control over many important factors, and for many chondro keepers it is an option that pays off well.

Cage Design

When it all boils down, a snake cage is a heated box, and that box must include consideration for the kind of heater that will be used. The introduction of heat panels has greatly simplified this. Besides the construction materials and heater type, factors such as size, shape, access, ventilation, visibility, and appearance all affect cage design, and impact the needs of the snakes and keepers in various ways. I divide these into three areas: The needs of the animals, which obviously must come first; the ease with which the keeper can provide these needs; and finally the personal preferences and tastes of the keeper. I am a person who needs things to "look" right, and this often makes me the butt of jokes from my less aesthetically minded friends who care only for function. However, I would never compromise or sacrifice the well-being of my chondros to satisfy a personal preference. I see too many keepers who reverse the priority of the design factors listed above, and place their own wants and wishes first. For example, I have shared correspondence with keepers who insist on setting up very large and elaborately planted vivaria for chondros, including small neonates. While I am quite aware of the appeal of such extremely attractive displays, and personally enjoy viewing them a lot, they are not in the best interest of the animals and good husbandry, in my opinion. Chondros are not decorations for use in "rainforest" vivaria. It is not necessary to sacrifice having a great-looking cage to be able to provide your animals with an ideal environment that is well-suited to their needs. The details of how to do this are covered in detail in the next chapter, but first let us examine all the important design factors that make good (and bad) cages.

Size

My personal rule of thumb for chondro cages is to provide as large a cage as is practical, and that you can reasonably afford. I need to qualify that statement by saying that it is possible to have too large a cage; and that "reasonably" is a very relative term. Cost should never be the primary consideration when choosing a cage, and it is my conviction that keepers have an obligation to spend the necessary money to provide good caging for their animals, even if it means having less animals. The size of your cages is important, because it will directly affect the heating and the heat gradient (or lack thereof), and to a lesser extent, the relative

This cage demonstrates all the elements of good design: Adequate size, proper shape, easy access, adequate ventilation, good visibility, and attractive appearance.

humidity of the cage environment. Cage size can also affect the activity level of your animals, ease of husbandry, amount of ventilation needed, and how secure your animals feel.

It has been stated frequently that a cage 24" by 24" by 24" is adequate for adult chondros, and this is most likely because a couple popular plastic cages are manufactured to those specifications. My feeling is that this size of cage is not large enough to permanently house mature adults (except some adult males, which tend to be smaller than females). I realize that there will be some knowledgeable keepers who will disagree with me about this, and will continue to use and recommend the 24" cube cage, but my purpose here is to inform you and to help you make the best decisions, based on what I have experienced and on my own judgments. Would so many people recommend this size of cage were it not for the fact that it has been aggressively marketed to those keeping arboreals, or that it has a nice "even" sound to it? I don't think so, and it is my opinion that most adult chondros will do better and breed more readily in cages that are somewhat larger. Therefore, the smallest size I would recommend for the average adult is a cage 30-36 inches long, 24 inches high, and 24 inches deep. Larger animals, especially mature females, should have a cage 36-48 inches long, and I consider this an ideal size for most chondros. Conversely, a cage longer than 48 inches or higher than 24-30 inches is excessive and can have disadvantages. Too large a cage can be difficult to heat, and too high a cage will require supplemental heat to ensure proper temperatures at floor level. It is also more difficult to humidify a larger air space, and smaller animals can feel insecure in an overly large enclosure.

You might ask why a larger cage is beneficial to an animal that "just sits there all the time". One of the many benefits to a roomy cage is that it encourages the animal to not just sit there! Lethargy and boredom are not the friends of captive chondros, and anything you can do to stimulate them and encourage exercise is important to long-term health. Small cages encourage the opposite behavior. They are also more prone to become stagnant, are soiled more quickly, can overheat more readily in the event of a problem, can become too warm when a florescent light is installed, and are visually less interesting and provide less opportunity for décor. Most importantly, it is nearly impossible to provide an adequate thermal gradient in a smaller cage. It is true that chondros can live in a cage with a uniform temperature as long as it is within acceptable parameters, but providing a gradient is highly desirable, and the wider the gradient the better, within acceptable parameters. Again, I realize that many have the attitude that chondros will be fine in a small cage with little or no thermal gradient. This is not how I approach things, and I feel my results speak for themselves. For example, rectal prolapse is not a common occurrence in my collection.

Shape

Shape can also impact important elements of chondro needs and husbandry. It is my belief that chondros benefit from cages oriented on a horizontal plane rather than a vertical one. This contradicts much of the advice given for arboreal caging. The utilization of tall cages may seem appropriate because chondros climb trees and shrubs, and because captive GTPs will frequently use the highest perch in the cage. This is more than likely due to the fact that it makes them feel secure, and it stands to reason that wild chondros may escape from threats real or imagined by being upwardly mobile. However, both wild and captive chondros will also take refuge on the cage floor and can be frequently observed prowling and resting on the ground. But the arboreal nature of GTPs has created a tendency for some keepers to utilize tall, vertically oriented caging. While this will not necessarily harm the animals, I do not feel it is the best design for a cage.

Many chondros enjoy using the cage floor as a resting place and this should be considered when choosing a cage shape and design.

It has been my observation that most chondros will ignore a vertical thermal gradient, and will select the perch that makes them feel most secure regardless of whether or not that location is within the ideal temperature range. In fact, many reptiles will trade proper temps for a hiding place that is too cool, if they feel exposed and must choose one over the other. As mentioned, for many chondros the most secure perch is the highest one, and they seem to gravitate to that location by nature. With a tall narrow cage shape, the chondro that prefers to roost high up will have to accept the temperature there, and it is difficult to provide a horizontal gradient in a tall cage unless the cage is both tall and wide. As has been pointed out already, this makes the cage excessively large and impractical, with too cool a floor level temperature. I consider the floor in my cages a part of the total environment usable by the animal, and this area should be warm enough, although it will usually be the coolest part of the cage. Tall enclosures are often difficult to humidify as well, because the damp substrate is too far from the heat source and simply sets wet rather than contributing to a humid cage environment.

Because of all these considerations, I feel that a longer, shorter cage is more practical, and is better utilized by the animals than a tall narrow cage. I prefer my cages to be shaped so that the entire cage can be accessed easily, with no hidden areas for the animals to hide or defecate in, and in such a way that the animals can use the entire interior.

Access

A good cage will feature easy and broad accessibility to the entire interior. A cage that is difficult to get into, or has limited access to some parts of the interior, is a pain in the keister and will be a source of daily irritation. This is one of the reasons why I do not like top opening cages, which in addition to being less than ideal for the cage environment are often not user friendly. A top door also requires approaching from above the animal to perform maintenance, and some chondros find this intimidating, and they may strike out of fear. Some cages open from the side, and this can make it difficult to access the far end of the cage unless both sides open. Such cages are also limited to placement in locations where the ends are not blocked by walls or other cages. I greatly prefer front opening cages, and there are two widely used types of doors: Hinged, and sliding glass. After using both types for many years, I have come to prefer sliding glass doors. The reasons include more controlled access, better visibility, the convenience of not having an open door to contend with when cleaning and feeding, ease of cage construction, and often less weight. Sliding glass allows the keeper to have very controlled, incremental access to one-half or even less of the cage interior, while a door requires all of the cage to be exposed at once, and also requires space to swing open which can be an issue in tight areas. Glass doors have no frame to block the view of the cage interior, and can be lifted out and removed for easy access when cleaning or stripping down the cage. On the down side, sliding glass doors can be more prone to accidental breakage and are a bit less secure, although neither concern is a problem when proper care is exercised.

Ventilation

Adequate ventilation is an important design element when considering chondro caging. Too little ventilation is unhealthy and will contribute to a stale, stagnant cage atmosphere that stays too wet and grows mold and mildew. Too much ventilation will prevent you from being able to maintain adequate humidity. Most commercial plastic cages have too much ventilation built into them, and in most parts of the U.S. the open areas must be partially covered to allow the relative humidity to be high enough. In fact, you will need to tailor the amount of ventilation in your cages to the local climate where you live, and even from season to season. In Ohio, where my home is, we experience wide shifts in the relative humidity from seasonal changes. I heat with wood, which makes the air in my house very dry, and in the heat of summer I use air conditioning, which also dries the air. The only periods of the year when my house has approximately the same level of relative humidity as the outdoors is the spring and fall. Consequently, I make adjustments in ventilation (and spraying cycles) to compensate for the current conditions. Details about this are covered in the next chapter, but we are concerned here with the principles of cage design that will allow such adjustments to be made, and that will make it easier to manage humidity.

A good rule of thumb is to plan for just a little more ventilation than you need, and then regulate it slightly. You will need to experiment with your cages until you find a good balance that allows you to build and maintain high daily humidity but still allows the cage to dry out overnight. If your cage has high humidity all the time, with heavy condensation on the glass, or mold and mildew developing on cage fixtures or the substrate, you may need to increase the ventilation, and/or decrease spraying cycles. Since most cage designs have rather generous ventilation, it is more common to decrease, rather than increase, the fresh air exchange to establish the correct balance. The easiest way to decrease cage ventilation is to cover up some of the cage openings with plastic. Heavy-duty clear freezer bags can be cut to size and used for this purpose, but any plastic heavy enough not to tear easily will do. Install these over some or all of the screened areas, using clear tape, on the outside of the cages. Experiment until you find the right balance. You can also build less vent openings into your cages if you make them yourself, after you find out what works well in your area. I recently began making my own cages with two vents rather than four, because I ended up always covering two of them anyway. Some vents have louvers or slides that can partially or completely close them off, making adjustments easy. If you need more ventilation in a commercially manufactured cage, you can usually drill small holes somewhere, or even cut out more openings and install your own vents.

There are many kinds of small plastic vents that you can buy for installation in chondro cages. The kind I use are made to provide cooling for audio and video equipment cabinets, where heat tends to build up to excessive amounts. They measure about 8 inches long and 3 inches wide, and have small non-moving louvers that no chondro could get through. Two of these do a good job in my cages, and I cover one of them with clear Plexiglas inserts cut to fit, in the driest parts of the year. You can look for vents in home improvement stores or hardware catalogs. Most are easy to install; you just cut an opening of predetermined dimensions and pop in the vent. Since warm air rises, some cage builders like to have vents at the floor level and at the top, with the idea that natural airflow will draw in through the lower vent. If you do this, make sure to keep the lower vents high enough so that spilled water and substrate material won't go through them. I like to locate my vents in the cage back rather than in the sides, because I locate many cages side by side, which would hinder good air flow. Some feel that rear ventilation is a poor choice if the cages are placed along a wall, as they usually are, but I have not found this to be a problem. The cages can always be placed a few inches away from the wall if there is a concern. Avoid locating ventilation in the tops of cages; the heat loss can be excessive, and top ventilation precludes stacking. Remember that sliding glass doors allow some air to flow between them, adding to the fresh air exchange inside the cage.

Most new cage builders tend to go overboard when allowing for ventilation, and many keepers have an exaggerated idea of how much ventilation snakes require. As noted previously, a stagnant cage atmosphere is to be avoided, but snakes do not need a huge quantity of airflow to be happy and healthy, and chondros will suffer if the cage ventilation won't allow adequate levels of humidity to be maintained.

Visibility

We keep chondros in large part because they are so beautiful, so it makes sense that many keepers place a premium on visibility when choosing caging. Visibility is more than just an aesthetic consideration however; it is important to be able to see well into the cage interior to perform routine husbandry and feeding tasks, as well as to make frequent inspections to determine an animal's well-being. As mentioned above, sliding glass doors provide slightly better cage visibility than hinged doors do. Visibility can be taken to an extreme, and I am not a fan of enclosures that expose the animals to view from many directions. I prefer to use real glass, of double strength thickness, in my cages. Plexiglas scratches easily and flexes excessively, so it's not the best choice for cage doors.

Appearance

There is no need to use unattractive cages, or those with bare, drab interiors. While many commercial cages are not all that attractive, in my opinion, they can at least be set up with an interior that is pleasant to the eye and healthy for the snake. On the other hand, custom made cages can be as attractive as the skills and budget of the builder allow. In either situation, complicated and elaborate cage plantings and decorations are best avoided. It is entirely possible to make an attractive "natural looking" cage interior that remains easy to clean and maintain - more on this in the next chapter. Dark cages tend to accentuate the colors of the snakes better than white cages and I feel that they tend to make the snakes feel more secure. The most important point to consider when designing the appearance of your cages is to keep the needs of the chondros uppermost in your thinking and let your personal tastes take second place if there is a conflict.

The author uses two sizes of tubs. These are shoebox sized tubs for hatchlings and three gallon tubs for yearlings. The racks provide warmth from thermostatically controlled heat tape that runs underneath each row of tubs.

Using Plastic Tubs To House Chondros

The comments of critics aside, plastic tubs make outstanding enclosures for chondros, and in fact are superior to any other type of cage for raising hatchlings and yearlings. Tubs do have a couple disadvantages, namely that they are top opening, and most are translucent and do not provide exceptional visibility from a display standpoint. However, the first issue becomes less of a concern when a rack is used to hold and heat the tubs, and tubs perform so well in every other respect that the visibility issue should be kept in perspective. The goal is to provide the best possible environment for delicate babies, and displaying them is not the top consideration. When you combine the low cost, ready accessibility of plastic tubs of many sizes, the ease of cleaning and disinfecting, and the ease with which tubs allow a humid environment to be maintained, it is hard to make a good argument against them.

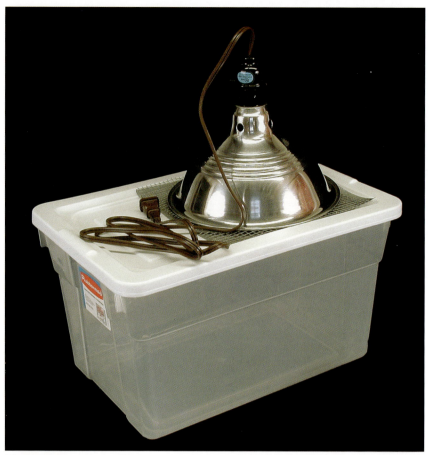

Single tub setup that is effective and inexpensive. Details for making this setup are on my web site. A thermostat and a thermometer are important when making any kind of tub environment for chondros.

You can set up single tubs, with heating and access provided at the top via the snap-on lid, or you can make or buy specially designed rack cabinets with built-in heat tapes that allow slide-out, lidless access to the tubs. I greatly prefer the latter because I work with large numbers of animals, but either method works well, and I have published plans for making racks and individual setups on my web site. See Appendix B for the address. Many keepers use an aluminum reflector with a red light bulb to heat individual tubs, placing this over a screened opening in the lid, but a small heat panel would work as well, if the tub were large enough. Drill small holes in the sides and ends of the tubs to provide ventilation. The quantity of these can be determined by experimentation. I drill 1/8-inch holes about an inch apart, in three rows, on all four sides of my tubs. When using lids with individual tub setups, it is a good idea to secure the lid at both ends with small clamps, available at office supply stores. I transfer my hatchlings from a "shoebox" size tub to a three-gallon tub when they are about six to eight months old, and from the three-gallon size to an adult display cage when they are about fourteen to eighteen months old, depending on individual growth rates. Even adults can be kept nicely in very large tubs, but once the animals develop adult colors, I like to place them in a setup that allows good visibility. When housing chondros of any age in plastic tubs, it is important to take the time to open each tub and inspect the animal at least once daily. Glass fronted cages make inspecting a group of adults much faster and more enjoyable and make a much better display, so I don't use tubs to house adults.

Chapter 9. Providing The Proper Cage Environment

"The history of life on Earth has been a history of interaction between living things and their surroundings."

Rachel Carson

Having well-designed cages that allow the keeper to easily provide for the needs of GTPs is an important first step in chondro husbandry. Understanding these needs, and knowing how to provide them, is the heart of the matter. In this chapter, we will discuss these needs and I will equip you to meet them. The information presented is based on an understanding and acceptance of the principles of good cage design that were detailed in Chapter 8, and therefore we will not cover ways to overcome bad design choices here.

Chondros are special snakes, and they have some specialized needs that must be met for them to thrive. These needs are not difficult to provide for, but they are not optional. Chondros come from a part of the world that is tropical, humid, wet, and equatorial. This means that they need an environment that is relatively stable, warm, with adequate hydration and humidity, and a balanced photoperiod; that is, approximately twelve hours each of day and night. They are highly nocturnal, so they do best when provided with a dark, relatively undisturbed night period. They are more delicate than many other kinds of pythons, and must be kept in sanitary conditions. Before we examine each of these topics in detail, it should be noted that the principles of good GTP husbandry in this section relate mostly to captive bred animals. Wild chondros may have differing temperature and humidity needs based on the habitat they came from. This is one possible reason why WC chondros often fail to thrive or breed, and why they are a poor choice for the average hobbyist. Such animals are best reserved for very experienced breeders who are equipped to deal with such challenges, and have valid reasons for doing so.

Temperature

Chondros do best when given a choice of thermal gradients within their enclosures, within a specific range. In the size of the adult cages that I use, and that were described in the previous chapter, both a horizontal, and a small vertical, temperature gradient can be established as long as the cage is located in a room that is sufficiently cool, but not too cold. I am not a fan of heated rooms, because it is not possible to provide much, if any, thermal cage gradient when the entire room is heated to cage temps. For this reason, I keep my chondro areas relatively cool, and provide my cages and tubs with a basking area. The cooler the cage location, the greater the thermal gradient that can be established, so long as the location is not too cool for the cage heaters to overcome. My cage location areas are about 72-78° F, unless I am cycling for breeding. This allows me to maintain cage gradients of approximately 75-90° F, with an average temperature of 84-86° F. Most chondros will seek out temperatures in this range as long as they feel secure. Some will choose cooler temperatures if they feel the location affords them more security. For this reason, it is important to maintain even the coolest parts of the cage at a safe minimum.

I don't like to allow my cages to be cooler than 75-78° F in any one spot, or warmer than 89° in the basking area. Again, an ideal average is 84-86° F. Individual chondros have individual thermal preferences which can change during feeding and shed cycles. To quote the children's nursery rhyme, "some like it hot, some like it cold". The important point is to allow the animals a choice, and make sure they are comfortable where they choose to spend the most time. A nighttime drop of a few degrees is acceptable, but not essential. Unless the animals are being thermally cycled for breeding, they should not be allowed to cool too much at night, with 72° F being a safe low point for adults. I keep my young animals warmer than this, and make no special effort to drop nighttime temperatures for animals of any age, other than when breeding. Some will argue that providing night time heat isn't natural, but the chondros will thrive without any night drop, and I feel I get a better breeding response when cycling time comes if the animals have been maintained without any night time cooling the rest of the year.

There are several types of heating devices commonly used for reptile cages, including light bulbs, ceramic heaters, heat tape and heat pads, and heat panels. Some keepers of arboreal snakes use heated perches, running a length of heat tape inside PVC pipe, but I do not recommend this. It provides no gradient and forces the animal to coil on a heated surface, which is neither necessary nor even desirable. If you use light bulbs to provide heat, use red colored bulbs because they will not disturb nocturnal cycles. Ceramic reptile heaters make maintaining an

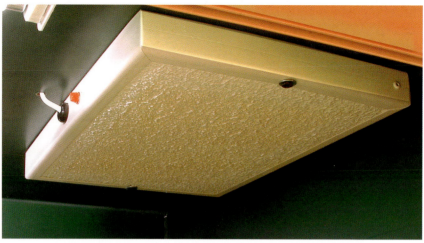

35 watt Pro Products® heat panel used by the author in all of his adult cages.

even temperature day and night easy, because they do not emit any light to interrupt the nocturnal cycle, but ceramic heaters can cause severe burns when used inside cages and have largely been made obsolete by the introduction of heat panels. In fact, heat panels are probably the only safe in-cage heating devices for arboreals. I use, and highly recommend, panels sold by Pro Products® of Mahopac, NY. See Appendix B for contact information. In my opinion, heat tape is best used for heating racks holding small tubs, and is excellent for that purpose. No matter what kind of heater is used, it is a good idea to use the smallest size, or wattage rating that will get the job done. This may prevent a fatal level of heat buildup or even a fire, in the event of a thermostat malfunction. Keep in mind that when using fluorescent lighting inside your cages the heat generated will raise the cage temperature several degrees.

Chondros do best in a stable environment, so locate cages in an area that does not experience wide temperature swings or drafts. Use proportional type thermostats that trickle electrical pulses to the heat device, allowing it to maintain a steady output, rather than mechanical on-off type of thermostats, which require a fluctuation of several degrees to actuate. "Wafer" thermostats that are sometimes seen on inexpensive incubators are an example of the latter, and should be avoided on both cages and incubators. When I say, "stable", I do not mean to infer static unchanging cage temperatures; rather, constant thermal vacillation and inconsistent cage conditions should be avoided. Adult chondros can sustain sharp drops in temperature, so long as they are temporary such as during a power outage in cold weather. Back-up heat or electricity must be in place for outages of more than a few hours. Younger animals with less developed immune systems should never be subjected to drastic drops in temperature.

Humidity

This is perhaps the most intimidating and confusing aspect of chondro husbandry for new or prospective owners, and a plethora of questionable advice via the Internet has not helped to resolve the issue. Judging and providing adequate humidity is one of those things that can be quite worrisome to the inexperienced keeper, but once some experience is gained, many realize that the humidity issue is not one to lose sleep over. The fact is, while chondros need moderate humidity levels to do well, and will suffer eventually if kept too dry, the exact amount of humidity is not critical. After all, relative humidity is "relative". Humidity is the measure of water vapor in the air, and different air temperatures can hold different amounts of water vapor. Warmer air can hold more water vapor than cooler air. This is why it is impractical to give specific percentages of humidity, unlike specifying exact degrees of temperature. 85° will always be the same in my cage as it is in yours, but 85% relative humidity will reflect differing amounts of water vapor if our cages are not matched in temperature and ventilation. For this reason, I don't use hygrometers in my cages, or strive to hit certain percentage numbers. It isn't that critical. By the way, cheap department store hygrometers are nearly worthless.

What you need to establish is a twenty-four hour cycle of high humidity followed by a drier period of moderate humidity. This is usually accomplished by daily misting or spraying cycles, as well as by keeping the cage substrate slightly damp, and these two factors work together with the amount of ventilation you provide. Keeping chondros too wet is as bad, perhaps even worse, than keeping them too dry. A constantly warm, wet environment can lead to unhealthy, stagnant conditions where mold and mildew can quickly develop, and skin fungus infections can take hold. Other than with delicate small hatchlings, and those of any age in a shed cycle, it is best to err a bit on the dry side, avoiding the unsanitary conditions of a sauna-like environment.

Temperature, ventilation, the amount of moisture you introduce to the cage via the substrate and daily spraying, along with the relative humidity inside of your house, are all factors that control how humid your cages will be. Since temperature is rather fixed within an appropriate range, humidity should then be regulated by finding a good balance between the amount of ventilation and the quantity of moisture added by you. There are no absolute formulas that can be provided because each situation is unique, and each keeper must discover, through some experimentation, the right balance for his or her own conditions. If your cages are dry, with no condensation or "fogging" on the glass three hours after you have sprayed them, then either you are spraying too lightly, or you have too much ventilation for the existing conditions. Conversely, if the condensation never goes away, or you are experiencing mildew or mold, then you are adding too much moisture, or your ventilation is inadequate. Often, adjusting both factors will bring about the best results, and as a general rule, it is better to have ample ventilation and spray more heavily, than to seal up a cage so that only light misting is needed. If you spray heavily and the cage dries quickly, the ventilation is excessive. It is also worth noting that just having wet substrate is not the same as having good humidity. I have seen cages with excessive ventilation that had sopping wet substrate but very low humidity. Remember, humidity is the measure of water vapor in the air, not how wet your cage is. For this reason, the practice of using water as a substrate to boost humidity is not a good idea, and introduces other problems… see my comments in the substrate section. However, a good absorbent substrate can greatly assist in maintaining good humidity between spraying. If you have your spraying-to-ventilation ratio correct, you should be able to thoroughly wet, but not

These cage fronts are showing a buildup of high humidity following daily spraying. This humidity level will slowly decrease over the next twelve hours or so.

soak, the cage interior, including the perches, substrate, walls, plants, and the chondros, and observe a building up of near 100% humidity for several hours, followed by a gradual drying off period that allows the cage to dry considerably, but not completely, by the beginning of the cycle the following day. I usually spray in the afternoon, but other than avoiding spraying at night, the time isn't critical.

The exception to this is for opaque animals. Detailed information about this will be provided in Chapter 10, but suffice it to say here that during the entire shed cycle but especially the last day or so prior to sloughing, chondros need to be kept at an elevated humidity level. This is especially important for hatchlings, which have a very thin skin that easily dries on them, potentially causing serious health consequences. In fact, I do not allow hatchlings to dry completely between spray cycles, although a fluctuating humidity cycle is recommended for them too. Once the animals are several months old and have shown some noticeable growth, keeping them damp at all times is not as critical. Except for very young chondros or those that are opaque, going a few days without being sprayed presents no big problems. If you are going to be gone from home more than two or three days, or if you have baby or opaque chondros, get a friend to spray for you, having them perform the duty at least once with you present so they can get a feel for the proper technique. Having such a person can ease a lot of stress when you need to be gone.

I am not a big fan of automatic misting systems, or in-cage waterfalls, foggers, or bubbling devices. These things can all malfunction, and in my experience with misting systems, can require more maintenance than they are worth. Also, running such devices in multiple cages can be problematic, because no two cages will need exactly the same amount of spraying, even if they appear to be identical. If you have a multiple cage setup, you will quickly learn which cages need a bit more moisture and which ones need a bit less. Also, misting daily by hand gives the keeper a time each day to check each cage and animal. Automated systems can encourage us to become lazy, and perhaps a bit sloppy, with daily husbandry. Nevertheless, some keepers like these systems and find them useful. This is a personal preference, and as long as the animals have adequate humidity and are shedding well, then what ever works best for each individual is good. If a proper relationship between ventilation and misting is developed and maintained, there is no need for special devices to introduce supplemental humidity. Remember: Simple is better!

Drinking Water

Chondros drink water two ways: From a bowl, and by licking drops from off of themselves or cage fixtures. Some animals prefer one method to the other, and some use both. Many animals are rarely observed drinking water at all, but still appear sleek and healthy, with normal moist defecations. Since any chondro may potentially drink water drops from off of itself, it is a good practice to make sure to mist directly on the animals during daily spraying, affording them the opportunity for a daily drink if they choose to take it. It is my feeling and observation that chondros, like most wild animals, are quite adept at sensing and locating water, and there is little chance of dehydration if healthy animals are given both a daily misting as well as fresh water in a bowl, and are housed in a properly humidified environment. Suggestions that chondros lick water from themselves because they are dehydrated, or that spraying chondros teaches them to "forget" how to drink from a dish, are without foundation.

Of course, using good quality water for spraying is as important as the water provided in the bowl. Unless you have really poor water, your tap will provide what the animals need. If you don't drink your tap water, it

"Buttermilk" (EB-95-31) is licking drops off of herself a few minutes after her cage was sprayed. You can see where her dry head and neck were buried in her coils while it was "raining".

may be a good idea to give the chondros what you use yourself. I use reverse-osmosis (RO) filtered water for both drinking and spraying, and while the results are not scientifically conclusive, I have noticed a virtual elimination of the kidney stress that I experienced occasionally in hatchlings, when I was using softened well water. Filtered water has a nice side benefit when used for cage spraying: it will not streak your cage glass with mineral deposits the way most tap and well water will. There has been some concern expressed about using RO or distilled water for reptiles, because of a lack of minerals in the former, and a negative electrical charge in the latter that is said to potentially leach good nutrients out of the animals' systems that drink it. It is my feeling that snakes get all the minerals they need from eating healthy prey items, and my animals have been thriving on RO water for over two years at the time of writing. I have never used distilled water, but other keepers have and have reported good results (Hickner, pers. com.). Still, it may be wise to buy spring water rather than distilled, as long as you are buying and have a choice. A Brita®, or other home filtering device, is an inexpensive way to provide quality drinking water for chondros.

Water bowls should be located in a cool corner of the cage, not over or under a heat source. Some keepers advocate placing water bowls on top of heat pads or heat tape to increase humidity. I don't care much for this approach, because who wants to drink warm water? Warm water also can grow bacteria more quickly than cool water. I feel it is best to provide cool drinking water, and to humidify the cage using the methods discussed above. The water bowl does not need to be excessively large. When I first began keeping arboreals, I used large plastic tubs for water, in the belief that this would help humidify the cage. All this did was make providing clean water more difficult, as the tubs full of water were quite heavy to carry around. This just tended to make me put off cleaning them and filling them with fresh water. A ten to twelve inch round bowl is fine for adult chondros, and smaller animals can have proportionately smaller bowls. Keeping clean water available for your chondros is much more important than the size of the bowl. Another idea that is set forth at times is the use of elevated drinking containers. In my opinion this is a solution looking for a problem that doesn't exist, and is rooted in a belief that chondros tend to be easily dehydrated. Since they spend most of the time perched in an elevated roost, the thought is that giving them an elevated drinking bowl will encourage them to drink more. First, I do not believe that when set up and maintained as described in this chapter, chondros have any tendency toward dehydration. Secondly I've never observed chondros having any problems finding or using water bowls. Your goal is to stimulate activity, and providing for every need right under their noses may contribute to lethargy. Who puts elevated water bowls in the trees for them in New Guinea? I see no need to do this, and it is one more idea that tends to complicate what is really a simple husbandry issue.

Lighting

Chondros do not seem to need any special lighting to be healthy, and will thrive in large tubs for years with nothing more than normal room lighting. They get all the nutrition they require from eating healthy prey items and do not need full spectrum lighting (or vitamins) like some reptiles do. There is some circumstantial evidence that exposing chondros suffering from respiratory infections to full-spectrum lighting may aid in a cure (Hickner, pers. com.), and using such lights does help provide a natural environment. There is a good reason to use full-spectrum lights in your cages aside from any possible health benefits: Chondros often look their best when displayed under certain kinds of full spectrum fluorescent lighting and in fact can appear to be much less colorful than they really are when viewed under some common types of indoor lighting. For example, the beautiful blue colors on some animals are rendered almost completely invisible by yellowish incandescent light bulbs. Normal white fluorescent bulbs also distort many colors. Any chondro looks its best when seen outside under overcast skies, or in the shade where the direct sun doesn't wash out the colors; this is "full spectrum" lighting in pure form. There are some fluorescent bulbs that closely replicate this lighting, and can help show your animals off with close to this natural outdoor appearance. I use a bulb made for tropical fish aquariums, and I have tried several others from a few different companies that gave satisfactory

18" fluorescent light used by the author in his adult cages. The harsh white light bulb is replaced with a full-spectrum bulb, and the plastic diffuser is discarded.

results. A few really boost one end of the spectrum and can create a purple or yellow cast to things, and I avoid these. I use low wattage fluorescent fixtures in my cages that use an 18-inch bulb and have an on/off switch that allows a timer to be used. Rocker, or "push, hold, and release" type switches can't be activated with a timer. Care must be taken to ensure that using such a fixture doesn't overheat your cage, as these units do put out some heat. This is one more argument against using small adult cages. In larger cages, the heat generated from fluorescent lights is much less of a factor.

Whether you use lighting installed in your cages for viewing or not, you should establish a twelve-hour photoperiod in the chondro area of your home. Since GTPs are from the equatorial tropics, they are naturally acclimated to a photo-cycle that is roughly divided into two equal halves; that is, twelve hours of light and twelve hours of dark. Near the equator, this cycle is in place year round and is not subject to seasonal changes like southern and northern latitudes are. While there is no hard evidence that I'm aware of that mandates this same cycle be provided for captive chondros, it does make sense to do so. At the very least the animals should have a consistent nighttime dark period of adequate duration, where they are undisturbed by ancillary lighting or much human activity. Being nocturnal, chondros are alert and in hunting mode when the lights go out, and some will be nervous and stressed by a lot of motion in front of their cages at this time. Others will strike the glass and possibly injure themselves, not out of aggression but as a result of the strong feeding response that most chondros exhibit at night, even specimens that are quite calm by day. The natural outside photoperiod where you live will probably affect the seasonal behavior of your animals unless you take steps to guard them from exposure to it. Most keepers do not, and there don't seem to be any repercussions from this, other than possibly affecting breeding activity or males going off feed in seasonal patterns. My observation is that these males will probably go off feed anyway, but I do see a more recognizable pattern of behavior in those animals exposed to seasonal variations in the natural outdoor photoperiod, than I do with animals in my main room that has no windows and is on a controlled twelve-hour photoperiod. All my cage lights are on this same schedule year round, regardless of any ambient or natural outdoor lighting. Use timers to provide a consistent daily photoperiod in cages and rooms, rather than manually switching lights on and off yourself. It is my opinion that manipulating the photoperiod artificially does not affect breeding cycles to any noticeable extent.

Substrate

There are many kinds of cage substrates that will work in chondro cages, including some that are manufactured specifically for use with reptiles. I have experimented with a few of these, and there are some recently introduced products that I have not tried. My own conclusion, and those of friends who have tried some of the products I have not, is that most of these are messy, or fail to perform successfully in one way or another. In my experience, there are two chondro cage substrates that shine above all others - newspaper and red cypress mulch.

Newspaper is cheap, readily accessible, holds moisture well, and is easily changed. It provides a sanitary, fresh cage floor covering each time it is changed. It can be folded or cut to fit cages or tubs. I use newspaper in all my hatchling and yearling tubs, and in my older adult melamine cages that would be compromised by continuous contact with damp mulch. The one exception to this is tubs housing yellow neonates, which tend to get black printers ink all over their faces when burrowing into damp newspaper. Printers ink, being soy-based, is harmless to reptiles, but it looks bad on yellow babies that are predisposed to rubbing their faces in the tub substrate. For these babies, I use white Bounty® paper towels. I like white towels with no dyed pattern on them, and Bounty is thick enough to hold up well and stay damp. Paper towels will grow mold faster than newspaper and will have to be changed more often if you use them, but they do keep little yellow faces yellow! I cut newspaper to fit my hatchling tubs on an office type paper cutter, allowing just a bit of excess so the paper folds up slightly in the sides and corners, which is where defecations often occur. A local store gives me all of their leftover Sunday newspapers, so I get all I need for free. Many stores throw away unsold papers once they cut the header off the front page for credit. Unless appearances are considered, I don't think there is a better cage substrate than newspaper.

My other favorite substrate is red cypress mulch, and I use it in all my adult cages except the few older melamine units. In my neck of the woods, this is sold by the pallet full year round, but especially in the spring, by every gas station and convenience store around. Cypress mulch is attractive, smells great, holds moisture wonderfully, is resistant to mold and insects, and is cheap. It is easily spot-cleaned when soiled. About the only negative thing that can be said is that mulch tends to be messy to work with, but a shop vac makes a quick job of cleaning up. There has been some discussion about the danger of chondros ingesting mulch or other similar substrate materials when eating, leading to

Red cypress mulch makes a great GTP cage substrate. It is available at convenience stores and nurseries year round in many parts of the U.S.

blockages of the GI tract. While I share the common concern most keepers feel about this, experience does not indicate that the threat is actual. Wild snakes must certainly ingest foreign debris when eating, and I have never seen an actual case of ingested substrate causing any harm to a snake in my care, extending back over thirty years. For more on this, see the feeding section in Chapter 10. I spot-clean soiled mulch and occasionally replace the entire cage floor with fresh mulch, such as when stripping down the cage for a new occupant, or when the mulch looks old and stale.

I avoid using substrates that are overly messy, tend to pack down and lose absorbency, absorb odors readily, grow mold quickly, stick to food items readily, do not hold moisture well, or may be toxic. These include, but are not limited to: Pea gravel, corncob bedding, pine shavings, cedar products, soil, and chunk type bark mulch. Also I do not advocate the use of water as a substrate. Somewhere the idea got started that the best way to keep arboreals is over standing water. This is a bad idea because it is difficult to keep the water clean and creates a circumstance where polluted water can easily be ingested by the animals. It also makes a humidity regimen nearly impossible to establish by creating a steam bath effect when limited ventilation is provided, and poor humidity when ventilation is increased. A wet cage floor is not the same thing as a humid cage environment.

Perches

Chondros, being mostly arboreal, need good solid perches of appropriate diameter. There are several types of commonly used perch material, and most work well. PVC plumbing pipe is commonly used for perches, and it is sold in several diameters. It is strong and easy to clean, and can be quickly mounted in a cage using end caps sold to match the pipe size. The caps can be screwed to the cage sides, and can be cut in half to make a cradle for the pipe that allows it to be removed easily. I confess to having a personal dislike for using PVC because it is so ugly, but it does work well. Wood dowels from the hardware store are also used, but I find that these discolor and mildew quickly in the humid cage environment. Some keepers try to seal them to prevent this, but I do not like my animals to have constant contact with chemicals, even if fully cured. See comments on film finishes in Chapter 8. Bamboo, acrylic, and fiberglass rods are also used for perches.

Natural wood branches make attractive perches for chondro cages and provide a variety of angles and diameters for the animals.

Natural wood branches are my perch material of choice for adult cages. I use Sugar Maple branches because they are non-toxic, locally abundant, grow in the sizes and configurations I need, and look very nice. I cut my branches from trees growing near meadows and clearings, because

Hook and eye hardware used by the author to mount branches in cages. These make the removal of branches fairly easy.

these trees have many low limbs that contain forks and side extensions that look nice, and allow a three-point installation that prevents rolling. I use only live cut branches, because insects may live in dead ones. I

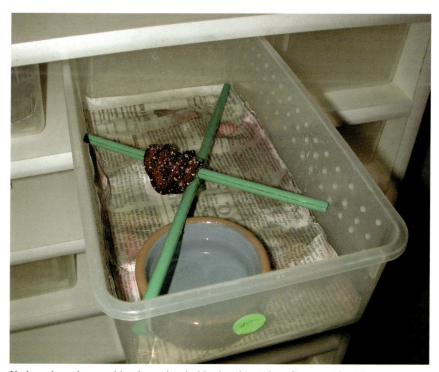

X-shaped perches used by the author in his shoe box tubs. Care must be taken to ensure that tails of hatchlings are not pinched when moving perches for cleaning.

153

Tic-tac-toe grids with the animals on them are easily removed from tubs for cleaning.

scrub new branches under hot running water with a stiff brush, and mount them in my cages using hooks and eyes, available from any good hardware store. The hooks screw into the ends of the branches, and hang onto corresponding eyes in the cage walls. These make secure mounts but are still easily removable. There is no need to bake such branches to sterilize them, when used as described. Natural branches look great, provide a textured perch that the animals feel secure on, and have varying diameters so the animals can choose one they like.

Perches must be securely mounted so they don't roll, slip, or fall under the weight of the animals. Use perches that are approximately the same diameter as the largest part of the snake's body that will be using them. Large adults should not be forced to use small diameter perches. An upper and lower perch will give the chondro some choice of where it wants to roost, but most chondros will select the highest spot in the cage. I provide a perch section under the heat panel for basking opportunities. If you install your perches so they are removable, you will thank yourself many times.

I have found that the best perches for babies and small yearlings are those made from plastic coat hangers. I buy bundles of these, and then cut off the long bottom length and the two shorter sides for use. For small shoebox tubs I make a simple X from a long piece and a short piece, using a zip tie in the center. I flex the X-shaped perch a little past perpendicular, and place it in the tub, where the spring action holds it in place. In my three-gallon tubs, I use a grid made of two long and two short sections, using zip ties to make a tic-tac-toe shaped assembly. Both of these are easily removed with the snakes still on them when replacing paper substrates and water bowls.

Plants

Plants make very attractive cage additions, and provide some welcome cover for the snakes. Live or silk plants can be used, depending on your level of commitment. Live plants must be pruned, watered, and fertilized, and must have temperature and lighting conditions suited to them that are not necessarily ideal for chondros.

Golden Pothos is a very common terrarium plant that is widely used in chondro cages. Some have great success with it, but after years of fooling with trying to keep it healthy and growing, I have given up and now use high quality silk Pothos. Probably my cages are not bright enough for Pothos to do well; even though it is listed as a low light plant, it does best when given a well-lit location, and in the tropics it grows wild in

High-quality silk plants look very real in cages and never turn yellow or die! Two types work well; these are dense bunch pieces on a single stalk, and long vines. The vines look great suspended from cage ceilings and add to the "jungle" look.

155

full sunlight. If you do use live plants, make sure to select a safe, non-toxic kind. All commercially grown houseplants have insecticide on them; so wash the leaves and stems well before placing them in cages. You may even want to repot them in new soil. Dipping the entire plant in a mild soap and water solution and then rinsing with clear water is a good way to get rid of all insecticide residues (Heller, pers. com.).

There are some very realistic looking silk Pothos and jungle type plants available at better craft stores. These are not inexpensive, but they generally hold up well and are easily disinfected. Cheaper synthetic plants may have green dye on them, which may wash off onto the substrate or perches. I use small round sections of florist's foam into which I insert the stems of my silk plants, burying the foam base in the mulch. I also hang vines from the cage ceiling, giving a pleasing "rain forest" look to the cages. Do not plant or decorate your cages so heavily that cleaning becomes difficult. A light to moderately planted cage looks nice, affords security to the animals, but is still relatively easy to keep clean. Keep in mind that mature males can become very active during real or perceived breeding periods and may tear up decorated cages during nighttime prowling.

Cleaning and Maintenance

It is a good practice to make a habit of checking your animals first thing each morning and the last thing each evening, at a minimum. Morning inspection includes a cursory check of cage temperatures, looking to see if any animals have defecated, especially in water bowls, and to make sure that all is well in each cage. Prolapse usually takes place overnight, and a quick discovery and treatment of this condition is essential to ensuring a good recovery. Some keepers spray at this time as well. Spraying time is not critical, or even important, and does not need to be performed to a set routine. After all, it doesn't rain at the same time each day. Mixing up the routine can encourage activity and help discourage lethargy. If possible, clean soiled cages when they are discovered, not just on "cleaning day". At the very least, clean out defecations the same day they are made, and immediately remove any water bowls that have been contaminated with feces, even if you can't disinfect them on the spot. Remove and record any sheds you find in the morning inspection as well. If you have fed the night before, pay attention that each animal actually consumed the food item, or you will have a most unpleasant surprise in 48 hours or so!

Common household chlorine bleach is a good general disinfectant and is

Items used for daily cleaning and husbandry include bleach, paper towels, Nolvasan (chlorohexadine), glass cleaner, scouring pad, and stainless steel scoop. Shelves on the left are good for drying clean water bowls and perches. The upper cart shelf holds a box of rubber gloves as well as shoe box substrate cut to fit. The calendar is handy for recording feed, shed, and breeding dates.

what I use to clean water bowls that have been defecated in. I soak the bowls with a diluted solution for ten to fifteen minutes, and then rinse them thoroughly before re-use. Follow the directions on the label for disinfecting with bleach. For most other cleaning chores, I use a commercial duty antibacterial cleaner, obtainable from veterinarians under several different brand names. I use a spray bottle to make up the cleaner from concentrate, and I use it to clean all non-porous surfaces, such as water bowls, plastic perches, tubs, and contact paper cage interiors. I use a scouring pad to scrub water bowls, then spray and rinse them. Water bowls should be disinfected at least weekly, and refilled with clean water. I use a big metal serving spoon to scoop soiled mulch, and I disinfect this after each use with the bleach solution. It is also a good idea to soak the scouring pad in the bleach after each cleaning session. Never use the scouring pad to scrub defecation stains, and then reuse it to scrub water bowls. I replace week-old newspaper in tubs with new, even if it hasn't been soiled, because after a week in warmth and dampness, it is no longer fresh. Finally, I use 409® Glass and Surface

Cleaner to clean glass doors. Always wash your hands with the antibacterial spray before and after handling animals, and after cleaning cages.

It may sound like my chondro facility is run more like a sterile hospital room than a snake-occupied basement, but in reality I just use common sense. Diseases and parasites are spread in fecal matter and on hands, so I pay careful attention to these areas. In their wild habitat, GTPs may be subject to natural parasites and predators, but they never have to lay in filth, drink stale contaminated water, breath musty stagnant air, or sit on a piece of pipe, with no stimulation, day after day. We should strive to provide a clean, fresh, stimulating environment for our animals that is both pleasing to us and healthy for them.

Chapter 10. Feeding, Defecation, and Shedding Cycles

"I have known many meat eaters to be far more nonviolent than vegetarians."

Mohandas Gandhi

In a recent ChondroWeb Forum poll, a majority of chondro owners indicated that feeding their animals was the most enjoyable of all the husbandry duties they performed. Indeed, there is something very satisfying about watching your jungle hunter come to full alert, seize its prey, and go to rest with a full belly after swallowing a nice-sized meal. Happiness is a room full of well-fed chondros! "How often should I feed my chondros?" is a frequently asked question, and I suspect that what more than a few keepers really want to know is "How often *can* I feed my chondros?" The answer to both questions depends on a number of variables relating to age, growth rate, activity level, and defecation cycles. The frequently given advice to withhold subsequent meals until the last one has been passed is not appropriate under most circumstances, and is based mostly on an inordinate fear of causing rectal prolapse. There will be more information about defecation cycles later in this chapter, but many animals will be underfed if you follow that regimen. But before discussing the important aspects of meal sizes and frequencies, let's look at some feeding basics that apply to all chondros regardless of age or size.

You Are What You Eat

If this were literally true, I would be a big stick of red licorice! Seriously, it is a well-known fact that what we put into our bodies directly affects our health, energy, and quality of life, and the same is true for GTPs. For this reason, the vast majority of captive chondros should be fed a diet of laboratory-raised mice or rats that have been fed a nutritious diet of high protein food themselves. In fact, lab-raised mice will consume their own young if the protein content of their food is too low. By "laboratory" I don't mean that only rodents bred and cared for by men in white coats in sterile, sealed buildings will do; rather, your rodents should come from a supplier who raises them in clean conditions specifically for reptile food, where they are not exposed to wild rodents, filth, or parasites. *Never*

Both the chondros and the keepers enjoy feeding time!

feed your chondros anything collected from a wild environment, whether it is rodent, amphibian, or other food. The risk of disease and parasites is too great, and not worth whatever reasons you may have for using such prey items. If you need to use lizards or frogs to entice your animal to eat, use these prey items to scent the lab rodent instead of feeding them to the snake. More about this can be found in Chapter 15, Managing Neonates. There is no need or reason to supplement a diet of healthy rodents with anything else, including chicks or other kinds of prey. Chondros get all the nutrition they need from the rodents and do not require any variety. Anyone who has experienced the feeding response of a hungry adult chondro will know that rats will do just fine!

Rarely but occasionally, an adult will refuse standard fare, and will insist on something unusual. Thomas Phillips, Webmaster of ChondroWeb.com, has a wild caught male that will only eat live Siberian Hamsters, despite the best efforts to convince the animal to accept more normal food. This is very rare with captive bred chondros, and in fact you could very well risk teaching your animals bad tricks by giving them supplemental food items that are not necessary. The practice of feeding chicks to chondros probably stems from the notion that birds make up a substantial part of their wild prey, which does not seem to be documented by actual evidence. Chicks make for rather nasty defecation by the snakes, and are a risk item for transmitting the bacteria Salmonella, both to you and the snakes. I would feed whole chicks only as a last resort.

The question arises as to whether it is best to buy rodents frozen from a rodent dealer, or to breed your own. I feel this issue is best resolved by considering whether you have more time, or money, to devote to the solution. It is far less expensive to produce your own rodents than it is to buy them. Furthermore, you have complete control over size, quantity, and the health of the rodent supply if it comes from yourself. If your collection is large, breeding your own rodents makes a lot of sense. But it does take a little time to maintain a colony, and it is best if the rodents are kept somewhere other than in your house. No matter how clean you keep them, rodents smell badly and there will be no doubt that they are in

It is easy to raise quite a few feeder rodents in a small space with a rack breeding setup and automatic watering system.

your home when you or guests enter. I keep my rodents in a barn on my property, and clean them once a week. It takes about two hours per week to clean, feed, and water them, and about $40-$50 per month for feed and bedding - far less than what I would pay to buy the same quantity I produce each month. On the other hand, it sure is wonderful to go to the freezer and pull out what you need with no muss or fuss (and no cleaning or smell), if you have the funds and are satisfied with the quality of the rodents your supplier provides. There are a number of good rodent suppliers around that will ship frozen rodents to your door, packed in dry ice. Many people are quite happy with the rodents and service they get from several of these dealers.

Producing your own rodents assures a constant supply of healthy animals in a variety of sizes.

Whether you buy your rodents, or grow your own, it is a good idea to feed frozen/thawed food to your animals. Freezing kills most parasites, although it does not kill all bacteria. In any event, always feed dead prey to your chondros whenever possible, which will be most animals, most of the time. Rarely, some chondros will only accept live food, and when this is the case, exercise extreme caution! Live rodents can be very aggressive, especially when cornered or in fear for their lives, and snakes can sustain severe bites and even fatal mutilation from being left unsupervised with live mice or rats. Often, unweaned live rats with their eyes still closed can be used and safely left in with the snake overnight, because they have not yet developed the ability to bite and attack. Such rat "fuzzies" also seem to be particularly attractive to recalcitrant feeders. Never risk feeding live prey to chondros for the "fun" of watching the snake make a kill, or for any other unnecessary reason, such as "to provide exercise". I quickly and humanely dispatch my live rodents by placing them in groups into heavy-duty freezer bags, and then squeezing out all the air. The animals quickly expire from lack of oxygen, and suffer less stress than when being stalked and constricted by a reptile.

The question has been raised from time to time as to whether rats or mice make the better meal for chondros, with a few keepers claiming that they observe faster growth rates when they convert to rats. My own observations do not agree with this conclusion, and I feel that individual chondros that are genetically predisposed to rapid growth will experience rapid growth regardless of which rodent they eat, as long as sufficient quantities are provided to support that growth. It is a fact of life that some chondros, like some people, grow faster and gain more weight than others do. I suspect that increased growth rates associated with feeding rats is actually the natural growth spurt that happens about the time young chondros outgrow mice anyway. It is also possible that those feeding rats to young chondros may tend to feed slightly larger meals, because baby and fuzzy rats are larger than corresponding mice. At any rate, I have observed that both slower growing chondros, as well as those putting on rapid growth, show the same growth rates regardless of whether they are being fed mice or rats of appropriate size.

Feed Me Now!

Chondros are all individuals, with individual food needs and feeding responses, but it is accurate to say that the average chondro has a rather enormous appetite. Exceptions to this include males that are off feed during seasonal fasting periods associated with the breeding instinct, and hatchlings that have not yet been established as feeders. There are also some slow feeders of both sexes, and of different ages, and these must be accepted as individuals on their own terms.

With the majority of GTPs however, you had better watch where you put your hands after sundown! In fact, some chondros have such big appetites that they would probably eat as much as you would feed them, even to their own harm. Meal size and feeding frequency must be tailored to each animal's age, size, and growth rate. The following are some general guidelines to use in determining what is best for your animals.

Unless an animal has a health-related issue such as a recent prolapse or regurgitation, you should feed it a meal large enough to make a noticeable, but not huge, lump in its belly. Chondros are equipped with that big maw for a reason, and they can take down a substantial meal. There is no fixed formula to determine prey size for a particular chondro, but it is not difficult to look at your snakes and choose mouse or rat sizes that are slightly bigger than the largest diameter of the snakes' bodies. I have seen inexperienced keepers fret over this unnecessarily - it isn't that critical. If the meal you feed doesn't make much of a lump, and the animal is prowling for food again in three days,

Feeder sizes of mice and rats used for chondros. Hatchlings start out on the smallest newborn mice pinkies and gradually move up to larger sized prey.

then increase the food size next time. If in doubt, feed smaller meals and work your way up, although you might be surprised to see just how big of a meal a healthy animal can take down and digest. But it is best not to push it too far. Neonate chondros start out on newborn pink mice, graduating up to fuzzy and "hopper" mice as they grow. Once an adult mouse doesn't make a full meal anymore, I switch them over to small rat pups, and from then on it is nothing but rats, which seems to be quite agreeable with the majority of chondros. A few animals reject rats for the first few times, and these exceptions can be weaned over by using some mouse scent on the rats until they get the idea. I make sure they learn this, because chain-feeding three or four adult mice to a maturing chondro is time-consuming and expensive.

In general, most chondros will do well on one meal every seven to ten days. I feed established neonates slightly more often, every five to seven days; and fully mature adults every ten to fourteen days. Yearlings in an obvious growth stage get nice large meals, because they need the food intake to sustain the rapid growth. When they slow down as young adults, I decrease meals accordingly. Chondros can appear to beg for food shamelessly, following your movements and engaging in caudal luring with enthusiasm. If an animal is growing very quickly, is defecating with regularity, and is engaged in nighttime prowling that is hunger related, then I sometimes offer food more frequently than normal. However, most animals will do best with a regular feeding regimen that is based on growth and age. Other exceptions include recovering postpartum females, males that have recently concluded a long seasonal fast, and to a lesser degree, females that are being conditioned for cycling and breeding. These groups get more food, again using common sense and good instincts as a guide.

Feeding Technique

Many chondros will only eat at night, and under dim lighting. You can use red cage or room lighting to see what you are doing, but in reality they don't need it to be quite that dark to eat well. I use a small incandescent spot light that I set on the floor and point at a corner away from the cages and tubs containing animals I am feeding. This lets me see quite well, but does not disturb the animals unduly. In fact, most of them are eagerly waiting for me. I use twelve-inch spring-type stainless steel forceps to feed babies and young juveniles. I find that using hemostats, with the scissor type action, does not give me a quick enough reflex to drop the pinky just as a baby grabs it, and I like the forceps much better. I use these to feed young animals until the strike range begins to get too close, which is usually about a year in age or so. At this time I switch over to a pair of fifteen-inch stainless steel hemostats that I use to feed adult chondros. I make these much more user friendly by using a grinding wheel to remove the locking mechanism, so that they open and close freely. Warning! Do not be tempted to use shorter tongs or implements when feeding adults, or you will donate blood. Chondros have heat-

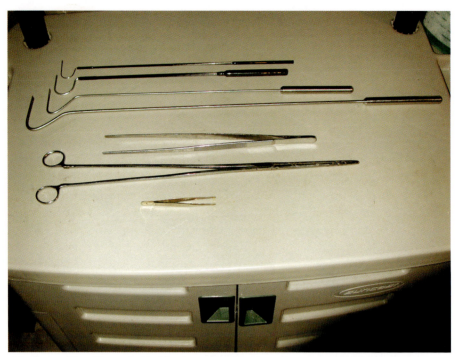

Feeding and handling tools used by the author. The large forceps are used for feeding hatchlings and juveniles; the hemostats are used for yearlings and adults. The small forceps are for assist-feeding mouse pinks to hatchlings. A variety of small and medium hooks are useful when handling chondros.

sensitive labial pits, and rely heavily on them to detect food, apparently even more so than scent. I learned this fact the hard way as an inexperienced keeper, and could not understand why the animals would tongue flick the presented rodent, and then reach out and nail my hand. When I switched to the longer hemostats, the problem was resolved, although there can still be close calls if you get sloppy. Be sure to open cages and tubs in such a way that your hand is not exposed to attack. By the way, I have never had my animals break teeth or do any other oral damage from being fed using steel feeding implements, and I have used them for years. However, I do recommend that you take care that your snakes don't strike the tongs, and I make sure to present food items so that they are seized by the head.

I thaw out my frozen rodents in tubs of hot water, rinsing them well to remove any droppings or bedding that may have stuck to them during freezing. You can also thaw rodents by letting them sit at room temperature all day, prior to an evening of feeding. If you do this, protect them from flies and other pests, and from household pets. A word of caution:

Do not attempt to thaw rodents by heating them on a heating pad or in the hot sun. It is easy to overdo it, which can severely weaken the abdominal wall of the food item. When the chondro grabs and constricts the item… well… it isn't pretty.

I offer the rodents still wet and warm from soaking in the hot water. The warmth makes the item more appealing to slower feeders, and the water helps hydrate and lubricate. Be sure to offer the item, in the tongs, at an angle that causes the snake to strike upward and then constrict without the food item hitting the cage floor, or the snake and food falling into the water bowl. This helps prevent the animal from ingesting any substrate like mulch, and from contaminating the drinking water with the rodent. If food or residue falls into the drinking water, rinse the bowl and refill. If you do see any substrate particles get into the chondro's mouth, you can attempt to remove them with small forceps while the animal is still swallowing the food. Do not attempt to reach into the cage once the food item is past the jaws and neck! If the animal does swallow small bits of substrate, there does not seem to be cause for alarm. I have never known this to cause any harm, after more than thirty years of using such substrates. Be very careful when feeding your chondros, or any time you

This is the safe and proper way to present food to a hungry chondro. Notice that the keeper's hand is off to the side of the cage opening and the prey is being presented to the animal head-first.

are working around them after dark, especially with a flashlight. Chondros are very alert at these times and aware of shadows on cage walls or the floor, and will sometimes strike at them risking injury or a mouthful of debris. Also, do not worry if your chondro occasionally chooses to swallow a food item tail first. For all of their relative intelligence, GTPs are not always very bright when it comes to finding and swallowing the heads of prey, and many chondros will grab a food item at mid-body regardless of how you offer it. Sometimes they can take seemingly forever to begin swallowing, but let them alone and usually they will get the job done. Rarely, you will have to present the item again, after they drop it.

Typical hanging coil of a constricting chondro.

Chondros usually swallow their prey head-first, but at times they will swallow the tail-end first.

I offer food to all animals of the same age and size groups at one time.

Off feed males and gravid females may be exceptions, but often are tried anyway. Most adult males from the age of fourteen to eighteen months and older will go off feed seasonally, and they will eat again just like they never stopped, when they are ready, not when you are. Do not get creative and try all kinds of strange food. If the male grew up eating rats, then he will eat them again when he is hungry. I work with problem feeders, which do not fall into the normal fasting patterns, at a different time than the rest of the collection, when I'm relaxed and can devote some focused attention to them. Tips for dealing with some of these issues are in Appendix A. Specific information for starting neonates is given in Chapter 15.

Do not recycle uneaten rodents for later use, and never offer a food item to a different animal if it has been in contact in any way with a non-feeder. Unless you are very experienced, never attempt to feed multiple animals in the same cage.

Defecation Cycles

Younger animals have a higher metabolism than older ones, and defecate more frequently, often depositing feces between feedings. At the other extreme, large mature females and even some males may go for weeks between bowel movements. Consequently, no hard and fast rules can be made concerning frequency of meals and defecation rates. The oft-repeated advice to wait for a bowel movement between each feeding is based on inordinate fears about prolapse, and doesn't hold up well in actual application. Many chondros will be underfed if this advice is followed. Personally, I feed my animals according to the schedule I have determined for them, based on their individual size, age, and growth rate. They get fed when it is time, whether they have defecated that week or not. Of course, an obviously constipated animal should not be fed, but just because an animal has not had a bowel movement in a while does not necessarily mean it is constipated. In fact, sometimes feeding the animal one more meal will trigger the next bowel movement. Chondros often defecate when shedding off their old skin.

Baby chondros often experience smeary, pasty defecations. One theory about this, and that makes sense, is that chondros are not used to eating pink mice, and may lack some of the stomach enzymes needed to digest them easily at first. It is assumed that neonates eat small frogs or lizards in the wild. Make sure babies are kept well hydrated as their systems adjust to a diet of rodents. Do not feed frogs, lizards, or other wild prey that may contain parasites to neonates. As the animals grow, they will begin to develop better-formed stool. Older animals should have well-formed, dark stool, along with lighter hair bundles, and white or yellowish urate deposits. This latter is the snake equivalent of urine, and is secreted by all snakes. Males seem to leave more urate deposits than females do, although females being courted by males during breeding periods may scent-mark perches and cage floors with small urate deposits. Odd-colored feces or diarrhea may indicate parasites or other health problems. If in doubt, have your vet perform in inexpensive fecal test, using a fresh stool sample. At the risk of being too graphic, I'll mention that chondro defecation can contain weird looking stuff at times, including orange granular looking matter, and gray or bluish urate material, and may be accompanied by quite a bit of clear fluid. If all else is well, and the animal has normal bowel movements in the future, there is no need to worry.

Some animals, in particular those that tend to "hold it" for a while, can develop the habit of letting the tail and part of the posterior section of the body hang down from the perch for several days prior to defecating. Such incidences of "tail hanging" often concern the keeper, and there is a general feeling by many that this behavior is indicative of constipation, and may precede prolapse. My experience is that usually neither is the case, and I have some animals that occasionally behave this way and always defecate normally with out prolapse. I do

Some adults, especially mature females, will engage in tail hanging behavior as seen here. Such behavior is rarely indicative of a problem.

pay attention to such animals and may try to stimulate them if I feel that is needed. I feed such animals a smaller than normal meal. Rarely is there any real problem, and most of these animals will have a bowel movement when they shed. For symptoms and treatment of irregularity and true constipation, see Appendix A.

Shedding cycles

Chondros, like all snakes, periodically shed their outer skin. Baby chondros normally undergo their first shed about ten days after hatching, and usually shed every six to eight weeks during the first year of growth. Rapidly growing specimens can even shed every four to six weeks. Chondros continue to shed throughout their lives, but the intervals between sheds are much longer in adults, due to a slower metabolism and lack of noticeable growth. Even old specimens benefit from renewing this protective outer covering, and shed a few times a year. Chondros that have been injured by a cut or tear of the hide will often undergo several sheds in succession until the wound is healed. Gravid females undergo a pre-lay shed approximately fourteen to twenty-one days prior to egg deposition.

This photo clearly shows an opaque, cloudy female next to her clear-eyed mate. Many color varieties do not show the opacity to this extent and it can be difficult to tell when they are preparing to shed.

171

Like all snakes, chondros go through a specific process while preparing to shed. The first thing that may be noticed is a normally good feeder refusing to eat. Many baby and yearling chondros will choose to accept food while preparing to shed, but most mature animals will not. A dulling of the normally bright colors follows food refusal, and in some cases a distinct milky haze will cover the animal including the clear scale that covers the eye. This milky haze is most noticeable on dark animals, especially maroon or brown babies, and may be very difficult to discern on yellow babies, to the point that inexperienced persons may find it nearly impossible to tell when a yellow neonate is opaque. Some adults develop bright salmon coloration on their bellies just before going opaque. After a day or two of peak cloudiness, the colors brighten again, almost to the point that everything looks normal again. After several more days, the animal will peel out of its old skin, turning it inside out like a sock being pulled off a foot. The entire process takes about ten days to complete.

Full sheds are a good indicator that your cage humidity is adequate.

Chondros must have adequate humidity to shed properly, and keepers are well advised to keep humidity levels boosted during the opaque period, and especially the last few days and hours prior to the removal of the skin. GTPs have very thin, delicate skins that easily dry on them during the final days of the shedding process. One of the most common beginner mistakes is not providing enough humidity during shedding, and it is wise to err on the wet side during this time, until you acquire a feel for getting it right. Full length, whole sheds are a good indication that your humidity is correct, although occasionally an animal may experience a bad shed even with adequate humidity present. This may be caused by poor health, or more commonly from stress of some kind. Even veteran keepers sometimes have to deal with poor or dried sheds, and detailed instructions for taking care of this problem are given in Appendix A.

Some chondros will begin accepting food again once they clear up from being opaque, but most keepers withhold food until the actual shed occurs. The last day or so before this happens, the old skin becomes very fragile, and it is vulnerable to tear prematurely if the animal is

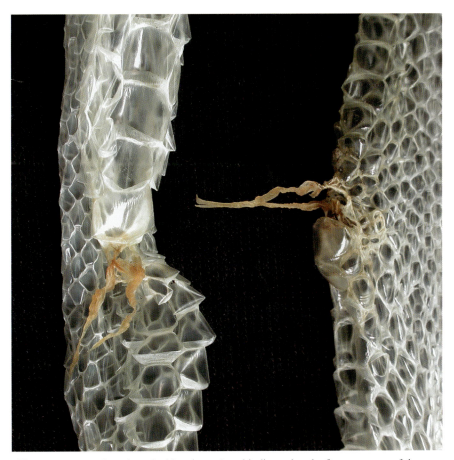

These are sperm plugs (not shed hemipenes) and indicate that the former owner of the shed skin is a male.

exposed to handling or anything abrasive. Scarring can occur if this happens too soon before the shed takes place. It is very important to not handle or stress the animals during the opaque period and right up to the final sloughing off of the old skin. Chondros may exhibit odd posturing, may choose unusual places to perch or lie, and generally act "under the weather" during the opaque period. The skin on the sides of the neck behind the jaws may also appear wrinkled or loose. Some chondros also exhibit a swollen head and nose during the opaque period, which lasts right up to the removal of the skin, and can be quite alarming when seen for the first time. This is apparently due to a buildup of fluid, but causes no harm and always clears up immediately after the shed takes place.

Chondros are resplendent with beautiful colors and iridescence after shedding, and this is a prime time for taking photographs. Since chondros often defecate as a part of the shedding process, and males sometimes shed out small sperm plugs with the old skin, this is also a good time to probe yearling or older animals for gender determination.

Summing It All Up

These wonderful and beautiful arboreal pythons are not necessarily right for every person who may want one, nor are they a good species for those on a limited budget, persons who travel a lot, or people too busy with other life issues to give chondros the attention and care they need. But we have also seen that they are not too difficult to care for, nor are their few but important needs overwhelming. For those who develop a passion that leads to commitment, success is a sweet reward, and chondros repay their owners many times over for the effort and energy we put into them. Many lives have been enriched, even changed, by these inhabitants of the rain forest. Their beauty and appeal is unique among captive reptile species, and rare is the person who's life has not been positively affected after having interaction with these extraordinary pythons.

Now, let us move on to the greatest challenge of working with chondros - the science and art of captive breeding.

Section III. Captive breeding

Chapter 11. The Challenge of Captive Breeding

"A special ability means a heavy expenditure of energy in a particular direction, with a consequent drain from some other side of life."

Carl G. Jung

Persons who have been deeply afflicted by chondroholism will experience no bigger challenge and no greater thrill than watching the noses and heads of their very own captive bred baby chondros poking out through the shells of closely watched seven week old eggs. I never get tired of breeding chondros, nor has my enthusiasm diminished with time, and each hatch is as exciting as the first one. I'll grant you that there is something unique about your first hatch, much like your first kiss… but neither thrill diminishes with time if executed properly. (Perhaps many of my readers realized just now how much of a chondro geek the author truly is!)

Baby chondros are the culmination of a lot of patience and hard work.

Persons who posses the skills and instincts required to consistently produce healthy chondros may come to feel that the endeavor isn't all that difficult; and in reality some aspects of captive breeding aren't considered as difficult as they once were. Still, it is generally accepted, and for good reasons, that chondros represent one of the more challenging breeding projects that reptile keepers can undertake. After all, if these things could be cranked out with the ease of most colubrids and even some boids, then captive bred baby chondros would be the normal offering of animal dealers instead of the imports usually seen. Especially amusing is the oft-repeated claim in Internet classified ads that the chondro offered for sale "will make a great breeder"! Aside from the fact that nobody can predict the breeding potential of individual chondros, much of this comes from people who have never bred a chondro in their lives, and find it easier (and more profitable) to sell imports and to broker non-feeding neonates, rather than learn to truly produce healthy captive bred stock. Chondros are not a commodity to be brokered and moved for the lowest price as quickly as possible; they are living jewels that deserve to be treated with respect and care, before and after the sale.

The steps to producing baby chondros escalate in degrees of difficulty as you get nearer to the final goal - a batch of healthy, established youngsters ready for new homes, including yours. (In fact, if you intend to develop a large collection, an important and pleasurable milestone is reached when you begin to "grow your own".) Inducing mature, well-acclimated adults to copulate is pretty easy to do; and getting a female or two to develop ripening egg follicles is not much more difficult, especially if you have several pairs breeding. Not all breeding females will ovulate, and some that do will produce only partially fertile clutches, and some only infertile slugs. Occasionally females will reabsorb the follicles and no ovulation takes place. Once a fertile clutch is obtained, then an incubation method must be successfully implemented. The emerging hatchlings must be carefully managed and set up, and once they experience their first shed, feeding trials begin. This last, critical phase, is what separates the "men from the boys" as the saying goes, and is why captive bred chondros will always be challenging to produce, even if all the other steps are reduced to a fool-proof formula (which isn't likely to happen either). Even so, I believe that anybody with enough dedication and patience, and having the right motivation, can successfully breed chondros. So much progress has been made, and so much helpful information has been made available, that breeding GTPs is no longer the lucky stab in the dark it was once considered to be.

This last fact bothers some breeders, and the truth is not everybody is happy about an increase in the success rate among newer breeders. I received much initial help from the written papers and oral advice of my friend Trooper Walsh, and I have always followed his example of being open to share information. I have not always been popular for sharing my own methods and results, or for articulating my own application of ideas developed by others. I think this sort of attitude is sad, and reflects not only a degree of selfishness, but also fear based on a lack of understanding about how market forces and free enterprise works. The root cause of most of the desire to hoard secrets and maintain exclusivity is greed, or a fear of losing income due to market saturation. My position is, and has always been, that the more success there is with chondros, the more passion that will be generated about them, and this will spill over to more people, fueling a consistent growth in the market. A policy of openness and honesty, serving and sharing, always pays more financial and other valuable dividends, than does the keeping back of information, the hoarding of secrets, and the attitude that others don't deserve the same satisfaction, joy, and rewards that some already have experienced. In defense of my position, I can cite the fact that the chondro market has only expanded and improved, with the value and demand for high-end specimens noticeably increasing, during the last several years since my web site was launched and the ChondroForums were developed. While I wish to make it clear that in no way do I take credit for all that has happened, and while I fully understand that many breeders and enthusiastic keepers have all contributed to the present realities, the two resources just mentioned have led the way in promoting the philosophy that I believe in, and I believe the results speak loudly.

The motivations for breeding chondros, like those for keeping them, are varied. Most are positive and constructive and are rooted in the same feelings of fascination and passion that inspire so many keepers. A few attempt to breed mostly for notoriety or a desire to make big money. Experienced commercial breeders smile a little to themselves when they run across one of these latter individuals, who has his yearly quotas and profit all mapped out, often before he has even produced his first clutch. In reality it just doesn't work that way, but some folks insist on learning this the hard way. If a hobbyist (and most breeders are hobbyists) is able to pay for his or her expenses, trade or sell to get new stock, and maybe make a little side money, then he or she is doing well. Chondro breeding is not a get-rich-quick proposition - if anything it is a "get-poor-fast" undertaking!

Critics often suggest that statements like these ring hollow when coming from commercial breeders, and from those like myself who work with

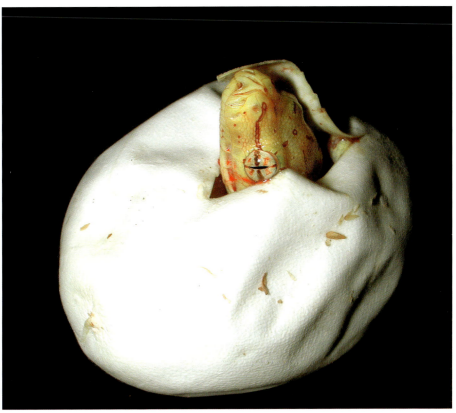

The best rewards from breeding Green Tree Pythons are not measured in dollars.

some very expensive bloodlines. For the record, I have no problem at all charging (and paying) top prices for extreme animals and rare morphs, and there is nothing wrong with charging top dollar for honestly represented top animals. However, I am drawn to these specimens first and foremost because they are ***beautiful***, not because they are expensive. I produce many mid and lower priced babies too, and it is the income from some of the more specialized morphs that allows me to do what I love for a living. I have said many times that if the animals I work with lost all commercial value, I would still work with them, because what fuels my passion for them is not money, but beauty and mystery.

I think the very best rewards from breeding chondros come in forms other than money, such as the indescribable sense of accomplishment, the sweetness of overcoming a challenge and achieving a difficult goal, the ability to develop your own bloodlines, and the independence of building a collection with your own efforts. With these rewards come the requisite responsibilities of establishing the babies and not just dumping them off cheaply because they present a difficulty; of keeping good records; of committing to providing your babies as good of a chance of survival as you are able, and to treat your customers, if any, in the same way you want to be treated.

While there is something to be respected about the methods of those who consistently produce quality babies, nobody should feel superior because of their success. There isn't one of us alive on this planet that has the power to create the spark of life, or has any infinite control over the results of breeding. Even veteran breeders have more failures, losses, and disappointments than they care to talk about, and anyone fortunate enough to experience the thrill of helping new little chondros into this world has many more people to thank than just himself… and we all must ultimately look to the Author of all life with gratitude for the privilege and the honor to be able to participate… and to cooperate.

Chapter 12. Conditioning and Cycling

"Having good health is very different from only being not sick."

Seneca The Younger

Successful breeding begins with a pair of conditioned mature animals in prime health and vigor.

Selection and Conditioning of Potential Breeders

The first requirement for producing healthy babies is to begin with healthy parents. Adult chondros being selected for potential breeders should be healthy in all respects, having had no medical problems for at least one year previous. They should be of good weight for their size, glossy, alert, and have good muscle tone. Males can become sexually active as young as eighteen months old, but females need to be much older and larger before they can be safely bred for the first time. The accepted rule of thumb is at least three years of age before beginning the first cycling

This conditioned female ("Chiquita", GM-99-01) has good fat reserves and is ready to begin thermal cycling.

period, *and* a body weight of at least 1000 grams. Smaller or younger females are subject to poor fertility, if they even ovulate. Females have a finite number of breeding periods in their lives, and it makes no sense to rush a female her first time, or to use up some of her energy and bodily resources for nothing. Patience is a way of life for chondro breeders.

The stress of cycling and breeding takes a toll on both animals, especially successfully bred females, which grow their ova (eggs) from scratch, undergo ovulation, and contribute the calcium needed to shell the eggs, all while enduring two to three months of fasting. Tack on another fifty days without food or water if she incubates the eggs herself. Males usually fast as well, sometimes much longer than the females, occasionally going seven or eight months out of the year without eating. For these reasons, it is important to condition potential breeders by feeding them up prior to the commencement of cycling. Females especially must have good fat reserves to undergo the strain that breeding activities put on their systems. It is generally acknowledged that most if not all snakes harbor potentially pathogenic bacteria in low numbers that are not a health threat under normal conditions. Stress can allow these bacteria to gain a foothold during a time of lowered immunity, and breeding necessarily stresses the animals. Respiratory infection (RI) is just one possibility under these circumstances, and while thermal cycling is commonly blamed for causing RI, it is far more likely that the overall stress of breeding activity is responsible for any health problems encountered at that time. RI is very uncommon in my experience when properly conditioned animals are cycled.

Potential breeders should be selected with genetic diversity in mind, unless the breeding is planned as part of a morph project that requires controlled inbreeding in attempts to establish or strengthen a trait. Sibling-to-sibling or parent-to-offspring mating should never be a matter of convenience to the breeder, and best results are often obtained from planning your breeding program rather than indiscriminately mixing and matching animals with the hope that something "takes". Potential breeders should also be established in your collection, well beyond the quarantine period recommended for newly acquired animals. Chondros are sensitive animals, and attempting to breed animals that have been recently purchased, or that have been frequently moved from cage to cage, often results in failure. One successful breeder friend of mine lost two seasons' worth of successful mating when he changed his facility to a new brand of cage, after many consecutive years of successfully breeding the animals. This is one reason why purchasing animals with the expectation of breeding them that same year is not a realistic idea, and why providing a stable, consistent environment is important.

I begin conditioning by increasing the meal frequency of breeder animals approximately two to three months prior to the anticipated onset of cycling. I prefer to feed smaller meals more frequently, rather than simply offering larger meals. Smaller food items are digested more easily and quickly, and I feel that this is the safest approach to extra weight gain. Obesity is always to be avoided, but some extra chunkiness on pre-cycling females is preferable. In fact, females without adequate fat reserves may not develop follicles. Since most females will eat ravenously at this time, beefing them up is not a problem. I like my males to be of good flesh at the beginning of the breeding period, but not especially heavy, because I think fat males make lazy, apathetic breeders. I continue to feed females on a weekly schedule throughout the breeding period. I offer food to the males as well, although most of them refuse food once cycling begins, and sometimes sooner. Cooler nighttime temperatures do not seem to pose any trouble for females with full stomachs, although I do keep meal sizes reasonable so as to not put any undue strain on their digestive systems. I feed females until they refuse food, which usually takes place as they begin to swell with ripening

"Blue Diamond" (AZ-95), one of the author's Sorong-type females showing the swelling associated with the early stages of follicle development.

follicles.

The second step in my conditioning program is to move the pair of breeder animals from their maintenance cages to their breeder cages. You will have to adjust this to your own facility, but in my basement I have a main room that houses most of my animals, and a cycling area outside of this room. It is not possible for me to drop the nighttime temperatures in the main room low enough for cycling because there are no windows, the room is insulated well, and most of the cages and racks need round-the-clock heat. My cycling area contains a small window, and by opening this, I can easily regulate the nighttime temperature. Consequently, I have to move breeders from the main room to the breeder cages in the cycling area, and one fact of life with chondros is that some of them, maybe most of them, don't like to be moved and will need an adjustment period. This can be the case even when seemingly identical cages are used, and I give my animals a few weeks to acclimate to the change before cycling and eventual pairing begins.

Cycling Regimen

The following cycling regimen is the one I have developed for use with the conditions and parameters of my facility and the climate where I live. There is more than one effective way to cycle chondros for breeding, and what follows works for me and serves to illustrate the fundamental principles involved. Each breeder will need to adapt these principles to his or her own situation. Although there are a few individuals in the U.S. who use little or no thermal cycling to induce breeding, I am not aware of any such breeder who claims *consistent* success. There are a few scattered reports of persons experiencing successful reproduction in pairs that have not been cycled, including an accidental breeding reported to me by a hobbyist. However, most breeders use thermal cycling to induce successful breeding, and most attempts at breeding without cycling result in failure. At the very least, it does seem to be important to expose the animals to some distinct environmental change, with temperature being the most common and effective. As mentioned, RI is not a problem when dropping night temperatures as long as a normal daytime basking temperature is provided throughout cycling. This is an important point; chondros do not hibernate (brumate) like many snakes, and must not be cooled around the clock. Always provide them with normal daytime temperatures of 78-89°. There is no sound evidence that manipulating light cycles to shorten or lengthen the photoperiod helps with successful cycling; this is most likely due to the equal length of days and nights in the equatorial home range of these animals. Some breeders do like to shorten the daily photoperiod when cycling, and some increase the frequency of spraying in the belief that this artificial "rainy" period induces breeding activity. I keep my photoperiod on a 12/12 cycle year round, but I do tend to spray pairs lightly just before lights out, to stimulate activity. I also make sure to spray in the evening if local weather includes storm fronts. However, it is my firm belief that thermal cycling is all that is required for consistent breeding success, and methods that rely on other stimuli usually achieve sporadic results. There doesn't seem to me to be any good reason *not* to cycle, except for unfounded health concerns. If a pair of chondros aren't fit enough to be cycled without health issues popping up, then they aren't in breeding condition to begin with.

Once my potential pairs are in prime breeding condition and settled into their separate breeder cages, I begin to drop the nighttime temperature. I use timers to shut off the cage lights and the heaters, and to turn them on again in the morning. I give the animals a week or so of nighttime temperatures in the mid 70's, and then I begin to lower them to about 68° or so by opening my window an appropriate amount for existing outside conditions. I continue with this daily cycle for several weeks, and then begin to pair up the animals. If they are compatible and ready to breed, courtship and copulation will usually commence immediately, and will take place frequently over many weeks. There is no set length of time for the cycling period; I gauge what I do based on my observations of the animals and some pairs will cycle and breed for several months. In general, I will continue to thermally cycle and pair two animals as long as they are actively breeding, and sometimes longer if I feel there is still a good chance that breeding activity will resume. I stop thermal cycling and initiate nighttime heat

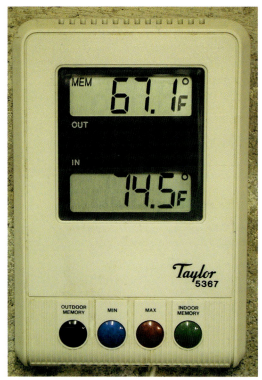

Nighttime lows of about 68° F are adequate for thermally cycling chondros for breeding. Indoor/outdoor thermometers with a memory feature make it easy to record the lowest temperature from the night before.

when: 1) I am convinced that the pair are completely done with any further breeding activity, that the pairing was not successful, and I do not plan on introducing a second male to the female; or 2) The breeding was successful and the female requires a return to nighttime warmth. Details about the thermal needs of gestating females will be given in the next chapter.

Since my cycling program is based on the existing local nighttime temperatures, I plan my pairings around the cooler months of the year. This makes for a longer potential breeding period than you might assume. Using only natural nighttime cooling, I have produced baby chondros in every month of the year except December and January, months that would correspond to cycling during the heat of summer. Since chondros are not seasonal breeders, and can be successfully cycled and bred as long as conditions are conducive, it is theoretically possible to use air conditioning to thermally cycle animals in the heat of summer. I have not attempted this yet. Since air conditioning can dry the air considerably, special attention would need to be paid to humidity levels if this method of cycling were to be used.

I have read comments to the effect that reestablishing nighttime heat is needed to induce females to ovulate. While it should be understood that there are several methods that have been successfully used to cycle and breed chondros, and no one way is the only "correct" way, I do not believe that the ovulation event is directly related to temperature cycles. In fact, many breeders do not understand the difference between follicle development and ovulation, and this will be covered in the next chapter. I'm convinced that it is best to continue thermal cycling for an indefinite period and to make changes according to observed results rather than arbitrarily establishing a pre-set length of time to begin nighttime heat again. Some females will show signs of progress in a relatively short time and others may cycle and breed for months. I once left a breeding pair together from March through August because they showed activity off and on during the entire time. Cycling for this pair began in February, and the eggs hatched the following November! Think in terms of months, not weeks, when planning cycling regimens.

Once I determine that it is time for the thermal cycling period to end, I simply remove the timer from the heat panel, and allow it to remain on throughout each twenty-four hour period, while maintaining the 12/12 photoperiod by keeping the cage lights on the timer. Males will usually commence eating within a short time of being separated from females and the heat being restored, but some will fast longer, beginning to eat again when they are ready. Both sexes are provided with the standard thermal gradient described in Chapter 9, regardless of whether the breeding has been successful. Males can be cycled again for future breeding, once they have had a resting period and have been eating for a few months, but don't push them too hard. Any females that did not become gravid may be cycled again, as long as they are given several months of stable thermal conditions and are well-fed and conditioned as described above. Any female that produces egg follicles should be given a full year of conditioning before being cycled again so as not to overtax her system. This is important even if a fertile clutch is not produced. Females that lay fully developed shelled slugs are as depleted as those laying fertile eggs, and must be given a full recovery period.

Chapter 13. Breeding, Ovulation, and Egg Laying

"Do a little dance, make a little love, get down tonight, get down tonight."

KC and the Sunshine Band

In this chapter we will cover the real "nuts and bolts" of breeding chondros, before going on to deal with incubation and neonate management in subsequent chapters. While cycling and egg incubation can be mostly reduced to formula and established procedures, the length of time and activities that take place between them are subject to variability and the individuality of the animals. A thorough understanding of the process and timeline can greatly assist the breeder in doing the right thing at the right time, as well as easing stress and worry about what is happening. I don't know about you, but I feel better knowing the facts, even if they aren't according to hope or expectation, rather than suffering the anxiety of being in the dark. Some of this core breeding activity can be aided or controlled by the breeder, but ultimately the success of each pairing is a matter of compatible, well-conditioned adults being paired at the right time, and of some things that we have no control over going well.

Courtship and Copulation

Usually, getting chondros to copulate is not difficult. Mature, sexually active males will almost always show immediate interest in mature, ready females. If they do not, all is not lost, but the odds of a successful pairing occurring during that breeding period with those two animals is not great, in my experience. Not all males are good breeders, and some males have a rather lackluster sex drive, and a few seem to have none. Other males, prized by their owners, might attempt to impregnate a hemp rope if placed in a cage with it! For this reason, it is a very good idea to have a heavy male-to-female ratio when setting up a breeding colony. Nothing is more frustrating than having a cycled, ready female waiting, and no interested males. In fact, I consider having a group of mature animals, consisting of no less than four or five males and three or four females, to be the minimum size and ratio to put the odds in the breeder's favor for obtaining one good clutch during a breeding period. Of course, all it takes is one pair to do the job, but we are talking odds here, not biology. There is a notable difference between "possible" and "probable", and those with only a single pair of chondros will be lucky to have success.

I like to introduce males to females in the late afternoon. Since males wander and can be quite active during the initial breeding period, it makes sense to me to allow a male to "find" a female.

Late afternoon introductions allow me to avoid

It is an exciting first step of your breeding project to have a compatible pair of chondros copulating. These two fine high yellows are in the Jeff Hudson collection.

a possible aggressive feeding response from the female, and puts the pair together shortly before the evening activity period is about to get underway. I often spray the animals at the same time I introduce the male. This may spark some activity as the lights go out, may help intensify scent pheromones from the female, and directs the attention of the animals to the water and the keeper, rather than at each other. While I definitely want the male to notice the female quickly, I also want to avoid an aggressive interaction in the first few minutes of co-existence. Two excellent times to make introductions are on days when a storm front and low-pressure system is in the area; or immediately after the female has shed her skin. Leaving the shed skin in the cage can help trigger interest, presumably due to the release of scent. There are times when I may choose to introduce a female to a male's cage; chief among these are when attempting to breed aggressive, territorial females that have a tendency to dominate males and defend a favorite cage location. Placing such a female in a strange cage can allow the male to get a few copulations in before the female re-establishes dominance and a new territory to guard. I continue this pattern of movement with such pairs, switching the female around to keep her off-guard. This trick was described to me by

189

Thomas Phillips, and was successfully used by him to obtain a clutch from his nasty female, the late "Endora", a wild caught Biak type that unfortunately didn't survive long after her babies hatched.

Not all pairs will be compatible, or receptive to breeding. Some females (and rarely, some males) will

"Barnose" (TW-94-146) is one of my best breeders and a "go-to" male when a backup is needed for a ready female.

seek refuge from a would-be suitor by escaping to the cage floor. Some females will become noticeably agitated, and will evert their cloaca, making a mess by smearing urates around the cage as they avoid contact with the male. This is not to be confused with the behavior, sometimes observed being performed by receptive females, of scent-marking the cage floor or perches with small amounts of urates. Rarely, one animal will show aggression toward the other. While this is very uncommon, introductions must be closely monitored to make sure that such an interaction does not occur. Chondros can inflict serious damage to each other with their sharp teeth, and such wounds can be fatal. Incidentally, *never* cage two males together! There is a possibility of them combating with each other, and this risk goes up considerably if there are any females nearby. There is no valid reason to house males communally, and to do so is irresponsible and risky. If your sexual pair doesn't show any aggression toward each other after an hour or so, then most likely they are safe to leave together.

If you observe any stress-related behavior from either animal over the next twelve to twenty-four hours, it is probably best to separate them and try them again a few days later. Do not force an animal to endure the stress and fear of being housed with a mate it clearly doesn't want contact with. If the pair seems to accept each other, but no courtship or breeding takes place, you can leave them together indefinitely, or you can separate them and try again in a few days. Sometimes the male will

These two photos show typical courtship posturing by the males. The draping of themselves over the females and attempted tail-wrapping are common displays, but no actual insertion is taking place. Such courtship activities usually take place promptly after compatible pairs are introduced, but may not necessarily result in actual breeding.

actively court the female, but with no response from her. Changing weather conditions, feeding cycles, shed cycles, and other unknown factors can all influence when pairs are receptive to breeding. Normally, however, a receptive female and a sexually active male will

191

Typical, entwined-tail position of breeding chondros. It is often very difficult to see if penetration is occuring and the mere act of tail-wrapping is not a guarantee that an actual breeding has taken place.

engage in almost immediate courtship behavior, culminating in copulation the first night they are together. Courtship activities include the male draping over the female, tail wrapping, the male titillating the female with his spurs, scent marking by either animal, the male following the female around the cage, and tail-raising by the female. Do not confuse tail wrapping with copulation. Actual penetration by one of the male's hemipenes, the paired copulatory organs possessed

Insertion of one of the male's hemipenes is visible in this photo. A small dental mirror is sometimes useful to help observe whether copulation is actually happening.

192

all male snakes, can be difficult to see with entwined, breeding chondros. Tails can be wrapped and the vents aligned without actual breeding taking place, and care must be exercised before a mating is confirmed. At times, a small reddish or purple section of an inserted hemipenis may be visible, and at other times the position of the tails may make this impossible to see. Sometimes it is clear from the contracted muscles near the vent of the male that he has engaged the female.

Copulation almost always commences after dark, but can last well into the following day, sometimes exceeding fourteen hours in duration. It is common for a pair to mate several times in succession over several days, and then seemingly ignore each other again. You can leave the pair together or separate them and re-pair them again in a few days. I usually keep my pairs together, often feeding the female in the cage while the male watches, himself uninterested in food. This requires experience and close observation to do safely, and if you have any doubts about your ability to pull it off, it is far better to remove the male. I prefer to disturb or handle my breeders as little as possible, so I don't usually split them up.

An exception is made when using the occasional male that will accept food during breeding (one of my best breeders does this), or when trying to stimulate activity in a slow male by removing him from the female. Often such males will wander their cages looking for the female, and breeding will resume once he is placed with her again. I let the male breed the female as often as he will, and for as long a period as he remains interested in her. Keep in mind that it is common for breeding activity to increase and decrease, and just because a pair has not mated in a few days, or even a couple weeks, doesn't mean they are finished for good. Shed cycles will definitely interrupt actively breeding pairs, and they will usually resume copulation immediately after a shed, especially a shed by the female. Copulations can number over a dozen, and take place over many weeks or even months. Unfortunately, multiple copulations do not assure a gravid female. One theory is that consistent breeding activity is an important trigger in stimulating follicle development in the female, so allow your pairs to keep breeding as long as they are willing.

Understanding Follicle Development and Ovulation

Female pythons grow their ova from scratch, and must have sufficient fat reserves for this to take place. This is in contrast to mammals, which are born with all their immature ova already in place. In pythons, ova are referred to as follicles until they are released from the ovaries, during an event called ovulation. The first real progress in obtaining a fertile clutch of eggs from a female chondro is made when she begins to develop ripening follicles. The symptoms of this usually begin to show after six to eight weeks of mating, but can take longer. These symptoms include a puffy or swollen appearance, a change in coloration that usually appears lighter than normal and is often bluish, going off feed, a personality change, a change in thermal preference, and a flattened or sunken appearance in the head. Not all specimens exhibit all of these symptoms, and going off feed, along with some swelling, are the two most reliable signs that something is happening.

This female is full of ripening egg follicles. Note the normal inner-looped coil and resting posture with the coils slightly rolled to the sides. The coils are flat or slightly hollow on the undersides.

Perhaps others are more sensitive to the "sunken head" effect than I am, but this has not been a common or easily observed sign in my experience. The number of developing follicles has a lot to do with how large an individual female will come to look, and in some females the swelling is not a reliable indicator, being no larger in appearance than normal fat reserves. Some females will seek heat during this time, and some will seek cooler temperatures. Making a thermal gradient available to the female is important. If a female is not seeking heat, I will continue with a mild nighttime temperature drop. If she is staying in the basking area, I will usually end the thermal cycle at that time, and restore full heat. As always, be sensitive to what the female is telling you she needs.

It is at this time of change and outward symptoms that many breeders believe their female to be gravid, but this is not the case yet. Certainly such females are on a course that will hopefully culminate in a successful breeding, and I use the term "pre-gravid" to describe females that are off feed and filling up with ripening follicles. However, until and unless the female undergoes a successful ovulation, she is not gravid, and may in fact reabsorb her egg follicles and return to a normal feeding and behavior pattern, leaving a very frustrated and confused breeder wondering what happened. "What happened" is that her ovaries reabsorbed the developing follicles, resulting in no ovulation and no clutch. The cause of this phenomenon is not clear, but there is evidence to indicate that failure to provide the pre-gravid female with sufficient heat can contribute to this problem. This was commented on by Walsh in a 1979 paper, and has been observed in my own collection as well.

Ovulation

Ovulation is the process of the ovaries releasing ripe follicles into the oviducts, where they are (potentially) fertilized and shelled. A normal ovulation is easy to observe once you understand what to look for, but Rob Worrell is generally credited with being the first to note that the ovulation swelling is observable in chondros an average of forty days prior to egg deposition. I've had females lay as early as thirty-eight days after ovulation, and as long as forty-five. A lot of early confusion resulted from a misunderstanding about what takes place during ovulation, and the difference between ovulation and follicle development, and at what point a female chondro becomes gravid; but today the process is understood and there is no need for anyone to be confused about what is happening with their snakes. The dictionary defines ovulation "to discharge ova", and it is universally understood that an animal cannot be gravid (pregnant) until ovulation occurs, because ovulation is the process whereby mature follicles (ova) are released from the ovaries for fertilization.

At the onset of ovulation, the female begins to break the ripe follicles free from the ovaries, and they are then gathered into the body cavity (Barker, pers. com.). Female pythons can sometimes be seen contracting the muscles as this takes place (Jannotti, pers. com.). Ovulation is accompanied by the quick onset of a very noticeable mid-body swelling that lasts from twenty-four to forty-eight hours, and disappears as quickly. Females show signs of being very uncomfortable during this short period, and ovulating females are usually quite restless and active, sometimes moving from one end of the cage to the other every hour or so, and almost constantly shifting positions. One thing that may be counted on during every normal ovulation is the large bloated area of the body. Females at the height of ovulation usually assume a characteristic stretched out posture, with the bloated area unable to flex over the perch

This is a classic ovulation swelling, with the lateral posturing that frequently accompanies the process. Ovulating females are restless and seldom hold one pose for more than 30 minutes or so during the 24-28 hour period.

and appearing stiff. This swelling is caused by the released follicles, now referred to as ova, being grouped up inside the female just prior to their entering the oviducts and being fertilized and shelled (if all goes well). Ovulation is an exciting event on the breeding calendar of the breeder, because for the first time since conditioning began, there is assurance that something is going to take place, because there is no biological mechanism in place for the female to absorb follicles once they are ovulated and shelled (Barker, pers. com.). Ovulation does not guarantee that fertile eggs will be laid, but it does mean the female is gravid and that the potential for a good clutch is present. Slugs may either be small, yellowish unshelled ova, or normal-sized, shelled ova. There is evidence that unshelled slugs may be reabsorbed, even after ovulation takes place (Crafton, pers. com.). An incident in my own experience tends to confirm this. Ovulation also marks the first date that can be used to predict the egg deposition and hatch with a fair degree of accuracy. Females that go longer than 45 days post-ovulation without laying eggs or slugs should be examined to determine if they are egg-bound.

The inexperienced breeder may have trouble distinguishing between a swollen female full of ripe follicles, and the ovulation event. After enough females have been observed in both conditions, the differences in behavior, posture, and appearance are pretty clear. Females with ripe follicles often sit very quietly day after day, and the swelling looks like a belly full of rodent. Such females often assume one of two common resting postures: One in which the body section containing the follicles hangs in a low loop just under the perch, much as an animal perches when it has eaten a large meal; the other is a tendency to roll the coils sideways slightly, especially when basking (see photos). While this is not practiced by chondros to the degree it is seen in

These two females are ovulating and may be distinguished from simply having ripening follicles by the size and shape of the swelling (round in cross-section), the rapid onset of the swelling, and the restlessness of the animals. Even the Aru-type, although ovulating on the ground, remained restless and shifted position frequently.

other boids, where the body may actually be inverted belly up, it is assumed that the function is the same - to expose the developing follicles to more heat. The coil containing the follicles can appear large and somewhat distended while on top of the perch and rolled this way, and some breeders mistake this for ovulation. Others confuse the low hanging coil posture for the ovulation swelling. It can be noticed however that when the coil is rolled sideways on the perch that the top of the coil may appear swollen and large, but the underside of the coil, where it contacts the perch, will have a slight hollow look to it. Ovulating females, on the other hand, are almost always very restless, shifting positions and perch locations; and the swelling is solid all the way around the body and belly, with no hollow area. It can look so large that one may begin to fear for the safety of the female, thinking she may burst!

I have mentioned watching for the signs of a "normal" ovulation. This is because female chondros do not always have a normal ovulation. In a textbook situation, the swelling develops quickly and smoothly, and has a peak time of several hours before smoothly reducing in size again. The process takes from twenty-four to forty-eight hours total, and appears to take a longer or shorter period depending on whether one or both ovaries ovulate. In my experience, the majority of females experience one ovulation of about 30 hours in length, but Worrell reports observing two separate events in many cases, as much as a week apart. This is assumed to be the second ovary releasing follicles some time after the first one, but the timing of egg deposition depends on the first swelling. If there is much deviation from this normal pattern and timeframe, including repeated small ovulations, no visible ovulation, a small ovulation swelling, or the peak swelling lasting too long or short of a time, then the result is usually either infertile slugs, a mix of slugs and good eggs, or a half-sized clutch of good eggs. Normal clutch size for an average adult female weighing 1200-1500 grams is about eighteen to twenty four eggs; clutches numbering nine to twelve eggs often seem to be related to less than perfect ovulation, and are assumed to be one-ovary clutches. With some experience, the breeder can usually tell from observing the ovulation if the clutch is going to be a good one or not. As I have learned, however, even this is not a guarantee of good results.

Preparing For Eggs

I always remove the male and restore heat to females once they ovulate, if I have not done so already. Gravid females will usually adopt a location that is suited to their thermal preference and gestate there without much movement. Gestation is approximately forty days, although it can range from 38 days to as long as 45 days, in my experience. Female chondros almost always undergo a pre-lay shed 14 to 21 days prior to egg deposition, and the timing of this event can be combined with the ovulation date to ascertain the likely timeframe for the eggs to arrive, accurate to within a few days. I have had females lay on day 14 and day 21 post-shed, but the average seems to be day 18 or 19. I have never had a female lay her eggs without having the pre-lay shed, and Walsh has experienced this once in twenty-five years (Walsh, pers. com.). With chondros, there are exceptions to everything, and there are records of females skipping the shed, but this should not be considered normal or common. I provide my females with a nesting box as soon as they complete the shed, if not sooner, although many females will not enter the nest box until just a few days before laying their eggs. I make my nest boxes out of pine, with a hinged top for easy

Nest box used by the author for gravid chondros. The design is based on one used by L. H. S. Van Mierop in early experiments studying the thermoregulatory ability of brooding females.

Females will often go through a restless period just prior to egg laying and may enter and exit the nest box for several days before settling in.

access, and a clear Plexiglas front for easy viewing. I cover this clear front with dark paper when not actually viewing the interior.

My boxes measure about ten inches square and are lined

Most females will enter the nest box for good at least 2-3 days before laying. The paper covering the front window has been lifted for this photo.

with a few inches of dry sphagnum moss. An access hole about three inches in diameter is made on one side. I prefer to mount my nest boxes

The author's female "Angel" laying a clutch of 25 fertile eggs. The brown spots are small areas of poor calcification and are usually not problematic.

with the access hole about perch height, but they can be set on the floor of the cage. The ambient temperature at the location of the nest box should be about 85-86° F. You can also use several other types of containers for nesting boxes, such as plastic ice cream tubs of appropriate size with a hole cut in the lid and dry moss inside. I hatched my first clutch of chondros in such a container using maternal incubation, but I have come to prefer wood nest boxes. They seem more natural, and females seem to like them better. For maternal incubation, they are also more thermally efficient than plastic.

Most females will enter the box several days before the eggs are laid, but a few enjoy the security of the box and will use it longer. For this reason, make sure it is located in a warm place in the cage, but not too warm. The use or non-use of a nest box by a particular female is not an indication of a successful or failed breeding. In other words, do not judge the status of things by whether or not your female enters the nest box. Rarely, a gravid female will not use a nest box and will lay her eggs in the water bowl or drop them from the perch. These females usually telegraph this behavior by acting restless and never settling down into the

The moment of egg deposition, captured through the front Plexiglas window of the nest box. Freshly laid chondro eggs have a translucent look to them and take a few minutes to dry and turn pearly white. Small yellow slugs are obvious, but shelled eggs must be candled to determine viability.

nest box. Females will often be in and out of the box a few times before making a permanent entrance into it, but females that are constantly cruising the cage as the date window for eggs draws near should be viewed with suspicion. My own practice is to seal such females in the nest box by day 14 after the shed, if they are acting this way. I have only one female in my collection that habitually refuses to lay in a nest box, but she settles down nicely once I seal her in by taping a piece of cardboard over the entrance hole. She will even brood the eggs normally if I let her. Restless females may choose to use a different type of nest box, or one in a different location, so experiment if you have a troublesome female. It may be a good idea to use a small water bowl to help prevent the female from laying eggs in it. Make sure to maintain an adequate humidity level for gestating females. Not only will this make them feel at ease, but will protect the eggs from desiccation while they are being laid.

In my experience, egg deposition usually begins early in the morning, before dawn, although it can take place at any time of the day. Females usually require several hours to complete the egg-laying process, and signal the completion of the job by forming up the clutch in what is called a beehive coil. This is a characteristic tight vertical coil with the head on top. (See photo in the Maternal Incubation section of Chapter 14.) The breeder will usually have made a choice of incubation method before the eggs arrive, and can now proceed with setting up the clutch for maternal or artificial incubation. Females with obvious retained ova must be removed from the clutch for treatment, and those few animals that will not brood their eggs make artificial incubation a necessity. We will look at both methods in detail next.

Chapter 14. Incubation

"When the press talks about my successes... hardly anyone mentions that I usually had more and better information than my colleagues."

Lyndon B. Johnson

There is no doubt about it; GTP eggs are one of the more difficult kinds of python eggs to hatch successfully. However, to say that some progress has been made in the last few years would be an understatement! Many new breeders are experiencing first time success, even with artificial incubation, once considered to be quite difficult. In this chapter, we will discuss both maternal and artificial incubation, and I'll explain all the details about successfully using either method, considering the pros and cons of each to help the breeder choose the best method for his or her particular circumstances.

Maternal Incubation

In the wild, female GTPs brood their eggs, and most captive females will readily do this as well. There is something very satisfying about watching a female brood her eggs, and it is an experience that I highly recommend for every breeder to participate in at least once. While I mostly use artificial incubation these days, for reasons mentioned later, I have a great fondness for maternal incubation. This is not only because of the high rate of success I enjoyed with it early on, but also because I understand artificial incubation better as a result of watching mom do it. I don't think that anybody can argue that mom doesn't know best! Maternal incubation is definitely the best choice for many new breeders, but it isn't foolproof. I have had several 100% hatches using this method, but also some dismal failures. Maternal incubation is kind of like a glass of cold milk- when it is good it is very good, but when it is bad, it is horrible. I'll share more about how to tell which direction a specific clutch is going later in this section.

Maternal incubation is easy and no expensive or fancy equipment is needed. If you are using a cage that can sustain continuous moderate humidity, you don't even need a brooding chamber, and can allow the female to incubate her eggs right in the cage where she laid them. The only conditions required for successful maternal incubation, once a good clutch is laid in the nest box and the female is willing to brood them, is adequate humidity and the correct ambient temperature. Notice I said "adequate" humidity, not high humidity. It has been stated that chondro eggs need close to 100% humidity to hatch, and this has caused some of those using maternal incubation to believe that the cage or chamber holding the nest box must be kept saturated. Not only is this a false idea, but it can also lead to unhealthy conditions for the mother and the eggs. Excessive moisture is a great enemy to chondro eggs, and many new breeders would be surprised to see the moderate level of humidity that will successfully hatch maternally incubated eggs. I use a large incubator for my brooding chamber for maternal clutches, and humidity is provided by tubs of water placed on empty shelves. Other than a light fog developing on the lower part of the glass door, no other outward signs of humidity are present, and hatch rates are excellent. Unlike chondros being kept in maintenance cages, I do not cycle the humidity for brooding females, but provide a constant, moderate level of humidity. Dripping condensation on the glass and mildew growth indicates excessive humidity levels. Also, it is important to make sure that the interior of the nest box remains dry at all times, both before and after egg deposition. The goal is a moderately humid chamber that is neither too dry nor too wet. Misting, large water tubs, and damp substrate can all help in maintaining an adequate humidity level. Also effective is a dampened bath towel hung over a perch, which evaporates moisture into the air. If you use this technique, change the towel as soon as a mildew odor is detected.

Experiments by many breeders have demonstrated that brooding female chondros regulate the temperature level of their eggs differently at different stages of development. If you provide her with an ambient temperature of 84-86° *outside* the nest box, then she will do all the work. Note that the temperature inside the nest box will be higher, due to the heat generated by the brooding female. The ambient temperature range stated will allow her to regulate her eggs with the least amount of expended energy. I lower the ambient temperature to the low end of this range in the final week of incubation, because females lower the temperature of their clutches then, and I want to make sure they have the ability to choose the temperature they want. Neither the humidity level nor the ambient temperature is super critical and as long as they are both provided within the ranges specified above, the female will do the rest. I once hatched a clutch of eggs that suffered through a three-day power outage, forcing the female to brood her eggs with ambient temps in the mid 70's until the heat was restored. All the eggs hatched.

The first thing to do when considering using maternal incubation for a specific clutch is to assess the overall pregnancy and the reproductive history of the female, if known. If the ovulation was abnormal, it is a good idea to plan on using artificial incubation because poor or irregular ovulation usually means poor fertilization. Females with a history of infertility or poor brooding instincts make mediocre candidates for maternal incubation. Once the clutch is being laid, try to candle a few of the exposed eggs (see Egg Management section in this chapter) to determine fertility and strength. The presence of any slugs or suspicious looking eggs indicates a need for artificial incubation.

Finally, observe the beehive coil of the female. A good mother will form up the clutch and hold it in such a way so as to control the environment all the way around the egg mass, even holding it up off the floor of the nest box. If the clutch is too large she may not be able to do this effectively. A flat, pancake-type coil is not good. (See photo below and on the next page.)

If a good female is provided with the correct environment, the factor that will ultimately determine the success of the incubation is the viability of the clutch. If the eggs are strong, and all are fertile, you will be setting up your new babies in 49 days. However, the Achilles' heel of maternal incubation is the presence of wet slugs. These are shelled but infertile ova that will begin to decompose at some point in the incubation process. Small, yellowish unshelled slugs are seldom a problem, and will harden and dry up, posing no threat to the good eggs. But, wet slugs can and will quickly ruin entire clutches once decomposition is underway. Such slugs turn bluish

The good, tight, vertical beehive coil being used by this wild Aru-type female is what you want to see. A good coil will lift the eggs off of the substrate and completely surround them.

205

green or purple, and will smell very foul. Detecting this odor can be the first clue to trouble, since the female will often not allow a very thorough inspection of the clutch once she forms up her beehive coil.

This female is attempting to brood a clutch of 24 fertile eggs, one of which can be seen in the front of the nest box. The clutch is too large for her to form up, resulting in a flat coil. The eggs were removed and incubated artificially.

I do not know if the presence of toxic gases contributes to the demise of good eggs, along with the contact moisture present when slugs are rotting, but I *can* tell you that failure to remedy the situation will very likely result in the death of all the good eggs. Other species of snake eggs can and do hatch when in contact with bad eggs, but chondro eggs are very sensitive, and will not tolerate such conditions, so ignore the skeptics who contradict this advice.

Since most females will not allow the removal of slugs from the clutch without a potentially dangerous battle, most breeders choose to pull the clutch if slugs are found to be present and finish incubating the good eggs artificially. Since there is always the possibility of this happening, an artificial setup must be ready at all times unless the breeder is willing to assume the risk. At least one person

These are slugs, but only the three smaller ones are visibly infertile. The large, normal-looking egg was determined to be infertile by candling and will begin to decompose in a matter of days.

These two infertile eggs are in the early stages of decay. Such eggs degrade rapidly in the humid, warm incubation environment and can turn wet and stink horribly in a matter of hours. Such wet slugs can quickly kill an entire clutch.

has claimed success with removing and then replacing the female while removing bad eggs, but I consider this risky. For one thing, slugs don't all go bad at the same rate, as anybody watching artificially incubated eggs can attest to, and I would not want to be continually removing the female to check. For another thing, the clutch might be affected adversely if you wait to discover whether a removed female is willing to re-establish her brooding of the egg mass. It is always a judgment call whether to remove a female and switch to artificial incubation, but at times the survival of the clutch will depend on it. I visually inspect the clutch as best I can by prodding the female into lifting a coil or two; this is done weekly, along with a daily scent check of the brooding chamber or cage. Healthy chondro clutches have a distinct, mild smell, but the harsh foul odor of rotten slugs will not be forgotten once you smell it. At the first sign of trouble, it is best to consider pulling the female. The entire clutch can spoil very quickly once decomposition begins, so move quickly if you decide to move at all. It is worth noting that occasionally, one or two eggs in an otherwise good clutch will turn dark purple or black, and sink in. Such eggs seldom smell or turn wet, and are not harmful.

The recent increase of success by those using artificial incubation has caused some bad press for the further use of maternal incubation, but I feel it can be the right choice for some. It is easy to do, and provides the enjoyment of gaining insight into yet one more fascinating and mysterious element of chondro behavior. It can mean the difference between success and failure in the event of a power outage if the breeder is not equipped with a generator, and it allows the breeder to be gone from home with much more peace of mind. For those not blessed with a detail-oriented personality or good egg care instincts, maternal incubation is definitely the way to go. And, it is nature's way. Maternally incubated eggs almost always hatch like clockwork on day 49 of incubation, and there is no greater thrill than seeing your female loosen her coils and watching those little yellow or maroon faces peer out at you. It is a mental image you will have for life.

A high white Aru type female guards her newly hatched babies. Photo courtesy of Chris Rouille.

Artificial Incubation

For a long time, the prospect of having to use artificial incubation to hatch chondro eggs struck fear into the hearts of breeders not experienced with it. Failures when using artificial incubation were well-known, and were more common than success. For years, Walsh and Bessette of Ophiological Services were among the few breeders who claimed consistent success in the U.S., utilizing a technique that worked very well for them, but unfortunately was not easily duplicated by others. This, and many initial failures with early GTP incubation attempts, led to the understandable conclusion that GTP eggs were extremely difficult to hatch using artificial methods. OS employed the use of large clear jars with screw-on lids to hatch eggs, with humidity supplied by damp pea gravel in the bottom of the container. This was covered with dry moss, and the humidity was regulated by the tightness of the lid, as well as the humidity level of the incubator. Once this closed system had the kinks worked out of it, success was obtainable, and I hatched my own first artificially incubated clutch using this method, but only after several failures while I learned to work with the method and my own equipment. The closed nature of this setup, and the lack of air exchange, seems to make this method intolerant of any deviation from ideal temperatures and humidity.

Eventually, other breeders including Tracy Barker, Rob Worrell, Jayson Flemming, Rico Walder, and Janet Hickner reported having success using damp vermiculite and different temperature regimens. To those having learned chondro egg husbandry from the pioneers of the subject, allowing the eggs to contact a damp substrate was considered anathema, and initially these reports were met with some skepticism.

The OS egg jar setup. Damp gravel is covered with dry sphagnum moss. Humidity is regulated by the tightness of the lid. Probes are inserted through a hole in the lid.

However, with high success rates being reported by several breeders, I decided to try the vermiculite method, tailoring the technique to my own equipment, and the knowledge and experience I already had obtained using both maternal and artificial incubation successfully. I had a near 100% hatch rate using vermiculite on two consecutive clutches. Around the same time, Trooper Walsh revealed a technique he had adapted from one widely used overseas, and by at least one other U.S. breeder (Gurley, pers. com.). Referred to as the "no substrate" method, the eggs are placed in a small dry container or a mesh net, and are suspended over water inside an egg box. This assembly is placed inside the incubator, which can be humid or dry. I tried the Walsh adaptation of this method with great success, and with some tweaking it has become my technique of choice. The vermiculite and no-substrate methods are detailed below. It is amusing to hear a few newer breeders scoff at earlier attitudes about the degree of difficulty in artificially hatching chondro eggs, now that easier methods have been worked out and published. Such persons may want to consider what artificial incubation was like before all the recent information was made available, and when answers were hard to come by and failure was common.

Artificial incubation has several distinct advantages over maternal, with the most important one being a much faster recovery for the female. This should not be used as an excuse to rush a female into the next cycling and breeding period, but it certainly does make things much less taxing on females, and probably results in a longer reproductive life for them. Other advantages include saving good eggs from contact with bad ones, and knowing the number, strength, and fertility rate of the clutch as soon as it is laid. Disadvantages include potential disaster from power outages, and the need for much more breeder participation and oversight. Artificial incubation is not recommended for those who are not detail-oriented.

Vermiculite

This absorbent mineral has been widely used for hatching snake eggs of all kinds for years, but its use for incubating chondro eggs is fairly recent. Worrell is credited with popularizing the technique, but a few other breeders have been using it for several years as well. To incubate eggs using this substrate, obtain some vermiculite from a garden supply store.

Mix vermiculite with water until it is damp enough to clump like a snowball. Squeeze out any excess moisture.

It comes in several grades, many people like a medium grade. Coarse can be too chunky and a fine grade may be too smeary and won't allow air to percolate under the eggs. I used a grade similar to coffee grounds for my experiments, and I would recommend a more course grade for those using this method. Vermiculite, being absorbent, comes with a variable amount of moisture in the bag; so quoting weight ratios of vermiculite-to-water is only usable if the vermiculite has been dried. A good place to begin is by mixing your vermiculite with enough clean water to make it moist, then squeezing out as much water as you can with your hands. The vermiculite will then be damp and clump easily, but will not be saturated and heavy. Place a two-inch layer of the vermiculite in a clear plastic box and drill plenty of ventilation holes in the lid. I like to use the type with a raised lid that makes extra air space; Hickner uses another tub placed upside down on the egg tub as a lid. Place the separated eggs on the substrate, embryos oriented up (see

Eggs being incubated in vermiculite. The eggs are slightly buried in the mixture and must be observed carefully to prevent too much swelling or desiccation.

instructions about candling in the Egg Management section), slightly burying them to about 25% of their height.

The eggs should stay nice and plump, but should not become tight or bloated. Eggs are porous and will absorb moisture during the course of incubation, and they can absorb too much moisture, even to the point of bursting. If the egg surfaces look stretched and taut, increase ventilation or replace the vermiculite with a drier mix. Conversely, if the eggs dent in, mist the vermiculite under those eggs and replace them; they should fill back out. I prefer to replace the vermiculite with fresh every three weeks or so during the course of incubation, or any time the mix is too wet or dry. I favor this method of regulation, rather than trying to add water to the existing mix. Let the eggs tell you what they need. Using vermiculite requires close observation and good judgment on the part of the breeder, but the method is not difficult to master once you get a feel for it. Be sure to keep an eye on the underside of the eggs as well as the tops, because vermiculite that is too dry can desiccate the eggs from the bottom. Note: It is normal for chondro eggs to dent in during the final twelve to fifteen days of incubation. This can be alarming to inexperienced breeders, but it is to be expected. Be sure to move pipped eggs to a hatch tub (see Chapter 15). Caution: Failure to do so when using a fine grade of vermiculite can be fatal to neonates, which can become coated with the stuff, and even choke on it. This is another reason to select a coarser grade of material over the really fine stuff. Using vermiculite is a hands-on, breeder participation method that requires a correct mix of water and substrate, and adjustments and maintenance along the way. It is a method that can result in first time success for those who use it properly, and there are breeders who swear by it.

The No Substrate Method

I like this technique because it removes the variable of determining the moisture content of the substrate and because it is nearly maintenance-free. This is the primary method of artificial egg incubation used in Europe, and it was also used by at least one U.S. breeder in the late 80s. It has recently caught on in the U.S. after Walsh described and published his technique for employing the method, on the ChondroForum. The setup is simple: An inch or so of water is placed in a clear tub and a plastic grid is suspended above the water using short sections of PVC pipe or similar material. The eggs are placed in small groups in dry containers such as deli cups, and these are placed on top of the grid. The lid is placed on the clear tub, and no ventilation holes are made in this tub or lid. The setup is then placed in the incubator, which is usually humidified. A light fog will develop on the lid of the clear tub, and some condensation will appear on the sides or front. The eggs will stay humidified but dry. I have never had a problem with water dripping on the eggs. The

This photo shows eggs being incubated in one of my incubators using the Walsh setup. Eggs are placed in deli cups and suspended over water on a plastic grid.

humidity in the egg box can be somewhat regulated by the humidity level inside the incubator. Air exchange is not important until the final stage of incubation, and I have successfully hatched clutches using this method without opening the incubator door for several weeks.

Materials used to set up eggs for my version of the Walsh no-substrate method. I have replaced the deli cups with one clear egg container and I place my eggs on plastic grids for complete air circulation. This allows me to incubate an entire clutch in one box.

However, the eggs will begin to emit moisture in the final twelve to fifteen days, and if adjustments are not made, the eggs can end up sitting in collected water. Providing extra ventilation via the tub lid is one way to

My setup, with eggs incubating. Humidity build-up can be seen on the front of the outer container. Note the thermostat probe and a thermocouple probe inserted through the front and in contact with the egg surfaces. Another thermometer probe (on top of the setup) records the external incubator temperature.

213

deal with this issue, and I make sure to dry the egg cups during this time.

Once the eggs pip, I set them up as described in the Egg Management section.

Incubators

An incubator is simply a heated and humidified box. There are commercial incubators available at both ends of the price spectrum, and while very expensive units such as the Forma Scientific® incubators, popularized by OS, are nice and have some very desirable features, there is no need to spend thousands of dollars for an incubator. I have seen GTP eggs die in them just as quickly as in a Styrofoam Hovabator®. A lot of people inquire as to which incubator is the most accurate, but in reality it is *consistency* that is important to incubator design and function. Accuracy means how close to perfection (when compared against a proven standard) a piece of equipment is; consistency means how much fluctuation in temperature and humidity the incubator will allow. As long as an incubator is consistent, I can calibrate out any error in the temperature read-out, but accuracy is nearly meaningless if the unit fluctuates too much. For chondro eggs, I define "too much" as anything more than 3-5 *tenths* of a degree Celsius. This is not to say that successful incubation temperatures must be that precise; but whatever temperature regimen you choose, it needs to be stable, and fluctuations of more than half a degree are too much and should be corrected before eggs are introduced. You can make your own incubator. There are published plans for doing so in the now out-of-print *Reproductive Husbandry of Pythons and Boas* by Ross and Marzec. *Reptiles* magazine also ran an article on converting an old refrigerator into an incubator, and some breeders are even using converted camping coolers. I use two incubators that I made myself, using Melamine. They are low-tech units but they never fluctuate more than two tenths of a degree once they are set, and usually they never change at all. Several companies market reasonably priced incubators, and most can be pressed into service for incubating chondro eggs.

If you buy or build an incubator made of any thermally efficient material, holding heat should not be a problem. It is important to use a good proportional thermostat, which trickles current to the heater and helps to maintain a very consistent temperature. In fact, your thermostat will determine to a large degree how consistent your unit will hold a preset temperature. Avoid mechanical on/off type thermostats, as these allow too much temperature fluctuation, often requiring changes of 3-5 degrees to actuate the heater. Wafer-type thermostats fall into this category, and should be replaced with a good proportional type. Humidity is introduced into incubators by the use of water reservoirs, whether built-in, or simple tubs you add and fill yourself. With both the vermiculite and no substrate methods, the eggs are kept in a humid egg tub; incubator humidity simply assists in maintaining the humidity inside this tub. A glass door is very valuable for observing the eggs without having to open the unit, which causes a loss of heat and humidity. *There is no one magic brand of incubator that will assure your success*, and most units will work if you become familiar with them and how they function in your home environment. Familiarity with your own equipment and how it behaves in your own facility is much more important than what kind of unit you use. It *is* important to place the incubator in a thermally stable location that is slightly cooler than the interior of the unit; this ensures that the heating element is always on, which contributes to consistency. Any incubator will struggle to hold a steady temperature in a location that is constantly changing.

My incubators are old CageMaster units; the smaller one on the left is the actual prototype I made. Humidity is supplied by the tubs of water on empty shelves. A flexible lamp is mounted on top for viewing and thermocouple probes can be seen inserted into the tubs with eggs.

It is important to calibrate all of your thermometers and thermostats against a known standard. These devices can all be inaccurate as well as inconsistent, and good equipment that is familiar to you is very valuable. By the way, calibration is not the process of adjusting your equipment until it reads perfectly. Rather, calibration means determining the degree of error for each piece of equipment so you can add or subtract that amount when reading a measurement from them. I use a laboratory grade, mercury thermometer than has been certified by a testing facility to N.I.S.T. traceable standards for accuracy. I calibrate all my other equipment against this instrument. For monitoring eggs, I use a thermocouple probe thermometer, placing the tip of the probe through a small hole in the lid of the egg box, and pinching it between two or more eggs. It is amazing to me that some people will put in the effort and patience it takes to get fertile chondro eggs, and then *hope* their temperature regulating and monitoring equipment is good enough to do the job. I know where mine is, to a few tenths of a degree, and I make sure it stays that way.

Egg Management

Of course, it stands to reason that in order to artificially incubate your eggs, you must first take them away from the female. This is a task best suited to two people, but I have done it by myself many times. Once the female has completed egg deposition and has formed up the clutch in her beehive coil, it is time to act. Remove the nest box from the cage, and open the lid. Some females will hunker down, and others will attack you. The important thing in the latter case is to move in quickly to prevent the female from damaging the eggs during striking. You can drop a small towel over her and quickly cover her with both hands while you find her head, or you can quickly grasp her head as soon as you open the lid, but either way, do it quickly. Cover calmer females with your hand and get the head under control. Begin to lift the female gently while attempting to unravel her from the egg mass, which usually will have begun to adhere together. This is where a second person is helpful. Try to free the clutch from her body and tail with as little vertical rotation as possible, and place the female into a prepared tub with damp substrate and clean water to drink, covering the front with paper if she is prone to striking at it. Good eggs are white and full, not small, yellowish, or sunken in. Some clutches contain eggs that are very smooth, while other clutches have what I call a "moon" surface… that is, they appear slightly lumpy on the surface, with snowflake-like spots. This is normal, and no cause for alarm.

Of course, you will have had your incubator and egg box set up and calibrated several days in advance of the eggs arriving. Now, separate each egg, candle it and mark the location of the embryo, and place it polar position up in the egg box. Separating the eggs is not difficult, but can be intimidating to those not experienced with it. The key is to go slowly, and very gently roll the egg being freed away from its fellows - don't simply pull the egg straight out. Some eggs will come apart easily, and others will take a bit of finesse. There will be a fuzzy textured spot on each egg

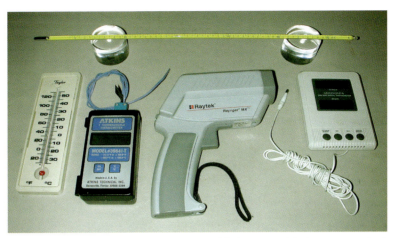

Thermometers used by the author include a certified mercury lab thermometer (top), and left to right: Taylor wall thermometer, Atkins thermocouple thermometer and bare-tipped probe, Raytek non-contact infrared thermometer, and a Taylor indoor-outdoor thermometer with memory. The custom acrylic lab thermometer holders are a cherished gift from a friend whom I guided through a successful first hatch.

where it was attached, but this is normal and doesn't hurt anything. You can leave the eggs adhered in small groups, but separating each egg allows you to remove bad ones easily, and if you manually pip the eggs later, it will be much easier to work with them individually. If the shell of an egg is ruptured during separation or at any other time, you can mend the area with melted paraffin. This is sold at grocery stores.

Candling is a step that has no direct bearing on successful incubation per se, but I feel it is important for several reasons, and I consider my candler to be a valuable tool. For those not familiar, a candler is a device that illuminates the interior of the egg by focusing a bright light against the shell, in the same way a flashlight held against your thumb makes it glow red. My candler has a flexible shaft with the light on the end. Candling establishes with a fair degree of certainty

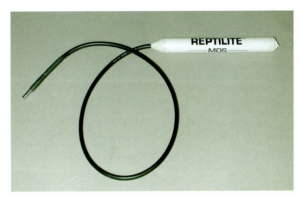

Reptile egg candler used by the author. I would not be without a candler.

217

if an egg is fertile, how strong it is based on the vein development, and the location of the embryo, which appears as a small dot or circle with veins emanating from it. The appearance is similar to the way highways originate from a major city on a map. There is some evidence that orienting the eggs with the embryo on top is important to normal

This poorly calcified fertile egg shows the network of veins that can be seen when candling a normal egg. Unfortunately, this egg did not remain viable. Photo courtesy of Marcial Mendez.

development, and I mark the embryo location with a felt tip marker as I candle each egg. I place any questionable eggs in their own cup when setting up the clutch so I can monitor them, and to remove the risk of them spoiling neighboring eggs while I'm away. I've seen non-viable but normal-looking eggs go from good to sour in a matter of hours. I'm able to anticipate this when candling reveals a yellow glow with no vein development. Healthy eggs have strong, visible vein growth when laid. Tiny veins or those barely visible can indicate a weak clutch, but these eggs usually hatch with proper conditions. Using a candler eliminates almost all of the guesswork and frustration caused by watching what appear to be good eggs suddenly turning colors and dieing.

Up until now, incubation temperatures have not been discussed. There is some variation in opinion about this, and some breeders use one temperature throughout incubation, while others follow the pattern established by monitoring brooding females. I am in the latter group, because "mother knows best". However, success can be obtained either way, and using one temperature can be helpful when multiple clutches are being incubated. I do feel that weaker clutches need the cooler incubation temps during the first week. Successful hatches have been reported using steady temperatures between 86° F (30° C) and 89° F (31.5° C). It should be pointed out that many breeders do not calibrate their equipment to precise standards; nor is it known whether these temperatures are egg or air temperatures. I follow the temperature regimen established early on by OS, and based on the careful monitoring of female thermoregulation of eggs. The eggs are established at 86-87° F (30-30.5° C) for the first week, then slowly increased to 89° F (31.5° C) for the next five weeks, and then cooled slightly to about 86° F (30° C) during the final

It is normal for eggs to begin emitting moisture and to dent in slightly during the last fifteen days of incubation. Provide extra ventilation during this time.

week. Eggs incubated at these temperatures will hatch in about 50 days. In closed incubation setups, there is evidence that the embryos will die full-term if the egg temps are not dropped in the final week, but this does not seem to be as critical in more open systems. It is important to note that the temperatures specified are egg surface temperatures, *not* incubator air temperatures. If in doubt, err slightly on the cool side. Eggs begin generating heat at a certain stage of incubation, and the egg surfaces will not be the same temperature as the surrounding air, especially if left in a mass. It is normal for the eggs to dent in during the final days of incubation.

It is my practice to manually pip any eggs that have not done so on their own by the evening of day 49 of incubation. This is the case whether I use maternal or artificial incubation. In almost all cases in my experience, maternally incubated eggs will begin to pip on day 49. When I see the first eggs pipping I pull the female and set up the clutch as described in the next chapter. Usually the female will have loosened her coils and you can see the slit eggs, and in some cases neonate heads. I begin watching maternally incubated clutches carefully beginning on day 48. Artificially incubated eggs often don't pip on day 49, and I always manually pip them if they do not. There is no doubt in my mind that this saves some neo-

Manually Pipping Eggs

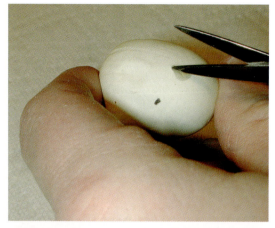

Using sharp-tipped, disinfected scissors, make a tiny snip in one end of the egg top. It is normal for a small amount of fluid and blood to seep from the incision.

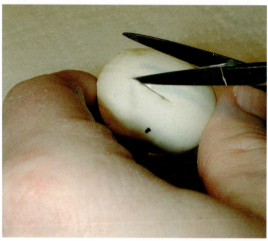

Making tiny cuts, extend the initial snip about 1/2 inch long. Keep the tip of the scissors pointed up, away from the veins that lay just under the shell.

Beginning at the initial snip, make another cut the same length as the first, forming a triangle with a base about 1/4 inch wide. The yellow neonate is just visible inside the egg.

nates from full-term egg death, and I have lost full-term neonates because I waited to pip the eggs. In a few cases, I have seen eggshells scratched where the neonates attempted to cut them, but were unable. Once I was observing a clutch on day 50 of artificial incubation and witnessed a neonate pushing the inside of the shell in an obvious attempt to cut through. By the time I got my pipping scissors and opened the egg, the neonate was dead. About half of that clutch was saved as I pipped the rest of the eggs, but the remainder were completely developed dead neonates. I decided then and there that never again would I wait longer than 49 days to pip eggs. At the very least, any eggs that have not pipped on their own within twenty-four hours of the rest should be cut.

It is important to point out that when done correctly, pipping the eggs does no harm to the neonates whatsoever, even if they are not quite full-term. Full pigmentation is the final development in neonates, and those that look a bit pale have a day or two more to go before emerging. I use sharp-tipped cuticle scissors to pip eggs, cutting a narrow triangular flap about ½ of an inch long parallel with the long axis of the egg, taking care to avoid cutting any major veins and spilling as little fluid as possible. Live neonates have a noticeable but slight reflex when touched with the tip of the scissors. Dead ones feel stiff and rubbery. It is not always easy to tell the difference, because the neonate will be under a lot of fluid and movement can be hard to see. Once I pip the eggs, I set them up, along with any eggs that have pipped on their own, in the tub setup described in the next chapter.

Chapter 15. Managing Neonates

"My mother had a great deal of trouble with me, but I think she enjoyed it."

Mark Twain

Congratulations! You have conditioned and cycled your adults, bred them, marked ovulation, obtained fertile eggs, and successfully incubated them. Now comes the most challenging and rewarding aspect of the entire process - the management of your new neonates, and establishing them as healthy, feeding animals that are ready for market. Be forewarned, dealing with neonates is *not* for the impatient or easily frustrated. Feeding them is a learned art, and as long as you have made it this far, why not develop the skills to do it? You can broker your animals to someone else, who may or may not get them feeding, but unless you have a trusted person of integrity to work with you on this, you owe it to yourself, the animals, the customers, and the industry, to put in the time and effort to establish your babies, and not simply dump them into the market and let somebody else worry about them. *There is a big difference between a broker and a true breeder.*

Neonate management begins by setting up the hatching eggs to allow the new babies to safely emerge. I set up full-term clutches in a clear shoebox-sized tub and lid, with damp white paper towels on the bottom, at about 85°. I do this once the eggs begin to pip, or after I manually pip them. Babies will usually stick out their noses or heads for a day before completely emerging from the egg at night, often just after the lights go out. My practice is to remove babies as they emerge, but they can be left in the hatch tub overnight. Most babies will have absorbed their yolk, but occasionally some will not and will weigh less than the normal hatch weight of 10-12 grams. Some babies will be dragging a bit of umbilical cord. Do not attempt to pull or cut this unless it is excessively long and appears to be giving the neonate trouble. Small lengths of umbilical cord will atrophy and fall off within 24-48 hours of emerging. If you need to cut a long cord that is attached to the yolk or egg, tie it off with a piece of dental floss first to prevent hemorrhage. Any young that have not emerged within 24-48 hours of the rest of the clutch may be deformed or have some other problem. Try to coax them out of the egg, but let them alone if all seems well. Euthanize any deformed babies by putting them in a plastic container and freezing them.

Hatch tub with the eggs pipped and set on plastic deli cup lids. These are placed on damp paper towels and the humidity is kept high. Neonates may be removed as they emerge or allowed to remain in the tub until the majority of them are out.

I have small plastic tubs all set up and ready for my new babies. These have a damp newspaper or white paper towel substrate, a small water dish, and a perch made of plastic coat hanger pieces. The gradient is set from 82-86°. As each baby emerges from the egg, I use a small hook to carefully lift it free of the hatch tub, and it goes straight to a triple-beam gram scale and the hatch weight is recorded. This goes onto a data card set up for each hatchling with pertinent data such as clutch and hatch dates, parentage, and the baby's hatch number. I use the system "GM-02-25" to identify hatchlings. This means Greg Maxwell is the breeder,

2002 is the hatch year, and this baby was the 25th hatchling that year. Then, the baby goes into its own tub labeled with its ID number, and with a colored sticker that identifies the bloodline. You may need to change the paper towels in the hatch tub once or twice during the hatch, because egg fluid and umbilical tissue can begin to smell quickly in the humid, warm environment.

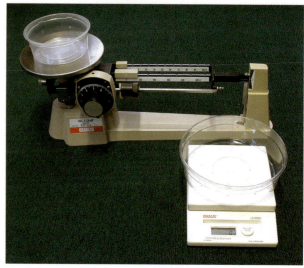

Scales used by the author. The balance scale is used for weighing neonates and the digital platform scale is great for yearlings and adults. Both can be zeroed to eliminate the need to subtract the weight of the container holding the snake.

Most babies will perch in the familiar inner looped position familiar to all chondro keepers, but some will prefer to lie on the floor of the tub. Some babies have a "tired" appearance, even laying their head sideways on the floor or on a coil. Most of the time these will be fine, and will recover and perch normally within a few days. Make sure to keep your newly hatched babies damp at all times, and never allow them to dry out completely. They will all shed about ten days after they hatch, and a good shed is critical to their getting a good start. Be extremely careful when handling hatchlings! They are very fragile. Never pull or stretch them, and always allow them to crawl where you want them, and off of hooks, perches, etc. I always

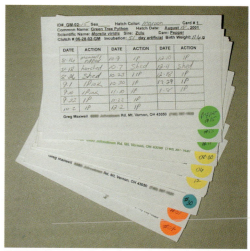

Data cards are made up for each animal. Customers should expect this information from the person they buy from.

say that as a rule-of-thumb, handle them as if they were made of wet tissue and you will avoid injuring them.

Feeding Trials

Some breeders offer food to new hatchlings right away, but I wait until they shed. They usually have bellies full of yolk when they hatch, and I like to have the best chance for initial

Nothing beats a shoe box tub rack for ease of caring for clutches of baby chondros. I color-code the different clutches with a numbered stick-on dot.

success when beginning feeding trials. Even established babies often won't accept food when preparing to shed, and I see no need to rush things with new babies. Once the clutch has shed, usually within a few days of each other, I do begin to work with them. I start out in late afternoon or early evening, with dim room lights and a bowl of hot water containing a number of thawed pinkies. I find I get the best strike responses from using warm pinkies, and I replenish the hot water as it cools, throughout the session. Use forceps at least 8" long. I prefer 12". These allow presentation of the food without the movement and heat from my hand being a distraction. Personally, I can't get the quick release I need to successfully feed difficult neonates when using scissor-type hemostats. The forceps allow a much faster release, and this is an important key.

I work with one hatchling at a time in its own tub, which I slide out of the rack about halfway, and begin by presenting the pink to it for inspection. Many babies will come to alert when disturbed, extending the front third of themselves forward and tongue flicking. A few babies will show interest in the scent of the pink and take it, but most will draw back. Holding the pink in such a way as to aid the snake in grasping the head, I bump the baby with the pink to elicit a strike. Some babies will strike and take the pink, many will strike and release, a few will refuse to strike, and occasionally a baby will drop off the perch and "run" as soon as you disturb it. Make notes of the responses you get with each baby for future use. Those that will strike, especially if they will hold for a second or two or begin to wrap the pink before they drop it, will usually not be much trouble. Non-strikers and runners are usually the most difficult to get feeding. I work with each neonate in turn, until I have success or I am convinced that it will not accept a meal during the session. This can be when the animal drops from the perch and thrashes, quits striking, or acts too stressed. This is a fine line to judge, and the majority of inexperienced keepers quit way too fast, and do not provoke the animals enough. I bump

This series of photos illustrates the actual first-time feeding of three neonates. After being poked with the food item, the baby chondro snaps at it. It is important to present the pinky in such a way that the chondro seizes it by the head. It may be necessary to repeat this step dozens of times before the neonate holds on.

them on the body, face, neck, and tail; I blow on them and chase them around the perch.

Sooner or later the animal will grasp the pink by the head, and may or may not wrap it up. When it does this, freeze in your tracks, because the slightest movement can cause the baby to spit out the pink. After what can seem like a very long time, the baby will begin to swallow the meal. It can take 10-20 minutes per animal, and dozens of strike and drops before the pink is held and

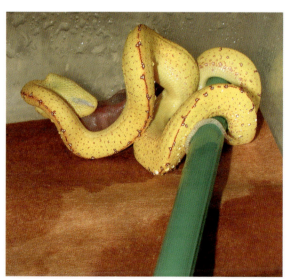

The moment the baby graps and holds the food, the keeper releases with the forceps and freezes. Some babies, like this one, hold the food on the tub bottom. Wait for the swallowing reflex to begin.

226

swallowed. It is important to try to end each session on a positive note with each baby, because I have found that both progress and stress can be cumulative; that is, the baby often remembers what happened in previous sessions. If progress was made, you can usually get back to where you left off fairly quickly. Progress can be defined as any small step that get closer to success. Striking, holding, wrapping, are all signs of progress, even if ultimately a meal is not taken that particular time.

Some neonates feed best while hanging with the food, and will release if they hit the tub floor. Not all babies will wrap the food item like this one.

Conversely, you can actually lose ground by over stressing the animal, programming it to react negatively the next time around.

After I try to get each animal to take a pink, I often go back and re-try those that refused the first time around, this time using a pink scented with chick down. Chick down is the light fluff a baby chick grows before it has feathers. I keep a frozen chick ready, and pinch off a small bunch of down for use at feeding time. Don't thaw the chick, just pinch off some down. Thawing increases the risk of

Down the hatch! Average sized hatchlings are fully capable of swallowing day-old pinkies. I save out the tiniest pinks for runts.

227

Salmonella growth, and makes the down wet and sticky. To scent, I dip the nose of a damp pink in the down to get a few wisps stuck in place. Offer the scented pink, trying to get the neonate to tongue flick the down. The response is usually immediate, if the trick is going to work, which it often does. I don't get into using a lot of different scents with troublesome babies until I have worked with them a while, and exhausted the possibilities for unscented and chick-scented pinks. After that, I try gerbil and hamster fur, in that order. One of these three scents almost always works for me eventually, except for the occasional hardcore "runner". Keep in mind the goal of scenting is not to make the chondro think, "Hey, I hate pinks but I love gerbil!" Rather, it is to get the animal to hang on long enough to begin to swallow, and just a little bit of hesitation instead of spitting out the pink can do the trick. Other scents sometimes used with success include small lizards, frogs, chicken broth, liquid "Lizard Maker®", and even rat fur. You may luck into something that works very well with a particular clutch, but don't be in a huge hurry to get creative; other than chick down I have not had scenting help all that much. It is not a miracle cure for the woes of starting new chondros, but it can really help at times. Whatever you do, do not feed whole frogs or lizards to baby chondros, because they can spread disease or parasites. If a baby will eat a frog, it will eat a frog-scented pink. It is my observation that most new breeders have trouble with technique, as opposed to lacking some magic-working scent. The two most common mistakes are expecting that baby chondros will recognize pinks as food, and failing to be aggressive or persistent enough in eliciting strikes.

Assist-Feeding

It can take quite a bit of work to get the majority of a clutch going, and often it takes 6-8 meals to begin to establish a decent feeding response without a lot of teasing required. I don't consider babies really established until they have taken a few meals with little or no effort, and it can take a dozen meals or more before they really start to get the idea. There will usually be one or two tough nuts to crack in any given clutch. I am not in a hurry to begin assist-feeding troublesome babies as long as they hatch with a normal weight. Such babies can easily go 8-10 weeks without feeding, although I may choose to assist-feed an animal sooner than that. I assist-feed a baby once I conclude that my best efforts just aren't making any progress at all, or I feel the animal is beginning to go downhill and needs nourishment to survive. It is important to note that assist-feeding requires skill, *and is not a quick fix, or a replacement for learning how to feed babies normally.* There is no reason to think about assist-feeding a healthy baby chondro any earlier than 8 weeks of age, and I often go longer. Assist feeding is stressful on both the keeper and the baby and can harm the animal if not done properly, but it can be the best way to save a few stubborn animals. I use small, blunt forceps to assist-feed whole tiny pinks, moistening them with water and inserting them in the mouth, then slowly and carefully pushing them past the rear jaw line and into the swallowing reflex area of the throat. The animal is quickly set on the floor of its tub and left alone to swallow the meal. If it doesn't I insert the pink again, pushing it as far down the throat as I safely can. Often a couple assist-feedings will jump start the baby to eating on its own, but I have had occasional babies that took over a dozen such efforts before finally accepting food. In my opinion, assist feeding whole pinks is much more beneficial than using a pinkie pump, both nutritionally and in advancing the goal of getting the animal to feed on its own.

I work with new babies once a week or so, waiting until I have a block of time to devote to the job, and making sure I am relaxed. Feeding new neonates is not something you take on at the end of a stressful day. However, there is a quiet satisfaction in knowing your little ones all have full bellies, and that you won! I can usually get about 60-80% of a given clutch to accept their first meals on the first or second try, and from then on it is a matter of working on the remaining babies. Give non-feeders several days to rest between feeding trials. Do not pester them day after day. It is worth repeating that starting chondro neonates is very much a learned art, and there is a curve to navigate before you will be skilled at it. There is a limit as to how far you can get by reading about it; it is far better to watch it being done by an experienced person if you are able. Ultimately, you must learn the finer points on your own, with trial and error. Breathe deeply, be patient, and believe in yourself… you can do it.

Grading Babies

I want to conclude this Breeding Section with a few comments on grading babies. There is a perception among some people that I possess a "magic" skill in choosing babies that turn into the best adults, and there is no denying that I have made some good picks, and have been very blessed! However, the most important ingredient in determining the potential of an offspring is its parents and other members of the family tree. I have made a strong effort to obtain offspring from some of the best bloodlines in the U.S., as well as developing my own. It's no wonder that some of my holdbacks have turned out the way they have, considering some of the parents I started with! Nonetheless, there is often quite a bit of variation within a given clutch, and while nobody has the ability to

The most important ingredient for exceptional offspring: Exceptional parents!

look at a group of babies and pick the best future adults from among them with anything approaching 100% accuracy, there are things that I look for when selecting babies for purchase, or to keep back from my own clutches.

It is important to wait until the babies shed before getting serious about choosing keepers. The first shed can reveal a surprising transformation in a baby, and color tones

This juvenile (GM-02-12), nicknamed "Darth Maul" because of its striped red head that resembles the Star Wars character, was selected as a Fine GTPs Keeper due to the unusual markings. It was also the only hatchling from the clutch with orange triangles.

and subtle markings that were not visible before often show well afterward. Maroon babies are especially prone to look much nicer after they shed. Once this happens, I look over the clutch to see if any babies really stand out from the rest. Several factors can contribute to a neonate being a standout, including having no markings or having a lot of them, high contrast between the body color and the markings, unusual color, unusually shaped markings, stripes, borders around markings… anything that catches my eye or looks unusual. One of my all-time best productions, "Calico Junior" (GM-99-09), was a very dark, almost black neonate with very few light markings. (See the photo in Chapter 4.) He was not necessarily the most stunning baby I have ever seen, but he was very unique and different, and that's what I look for. If all the babies in a clutch have yellow markings, and one has orange - then that one stays. If a clutch all looks pretty much the same, then you can select the larger babies. Some breeders select holdbacks largely based on feeding response or size. That makes sense if your main priorities are developing bloodlines that tend to large size or that feed easily. I haven't seen any conclusive data proving that keeping easy feeders produces more of them down the line, although it certainly may. I selectively breed for morphological traits; therefore, feeding response is of secondary importance to me. Give me the extreme specimens, and I'll happily deal with the feeding issues. (Ok, not happily… but willingly!)

Good Luck!

I personally wish you the best of success in your life with Green Tree Pythons, and with your own efforts to reproduce these wonderful and fascinating pythons in your own home. It is my sincere hope that I have passed on to you in these pages some of the passion I feel for chondros, and have stirred you to consider the ethics and responsibilities that come with GTP ownership and reproduction. I may have even irritated you with an opinion or comment here and there. If so, it was never my intention to be offensive, but rather, to argue for what I believe to be the truth, for what is important, and for what is honest.

We all have a great deal more to learn about these green snakes that so inspire us. Keeping an open mind and maintaining a posture for learning is important to making advances. It goes without saying that no one has a monopoly on knowledge or expertise with chondros, and you may be the person to contribute some new technique or gain a fresh insight into solving the many challenges this species presents us with. While there is no need to re-invent the wheel when it comes to the basics of husbandry or breeding, there is still much valuable work to be done. Have fun, enjoy your chondros, and always remember… *Quality is Contagious!*

Appendix A. Solving Common Problems

If you keep GTPs for any length of time, you will have a problem to solve sooner or later. That's just the reality of working with this species. I will briefly discuss some of the more common issues that eventually come up in the day-to-day husbandry of chondros. These are guidelines, and it is important to find a knowledgeable veterinarian that you can work with, *before* you need one. An excellent place to find a reptile vet is on the Association of Reptile and Amphibian Veterinarians web site (see Appendix B). It is beyond the scope of this guide to diagnose and offer treatment for all the possible things that can go wrong with chondros, but the basics are covered here to provide you with a good foundation for treating common troubles. Many of these are preventable with sound husbandry practices, but anybody can slip up now and then. The comments below relate mostly to outwardly healthy, captive bred animals.

Dry Sheds

Chondros are thin-skinned and prone to shedding problems if the humidity level is too low. With older animals, this is more of a nuisance than a health threat, but stuck sheds can severely stress and dehydrate small animals. Fortunately, the situation is fairly easy to resolve in either case. Place small snakes in a deli cup or small tub along with some saturated, wadded up paper towels. Make sure there is no more than 1/8 inch of water in the bottom to prevent drowning. Place the cup with the snake inside and the lid on in a warm place (84° or so), and the shed should come off within 24-48 hours. Cover the snake with the towel occasionally to encourage it to rub its

Setup for softening a dried shed on a neonate. Make sure that there is not enough water in the bottom of the cup to drown the baby.

way out, which will help the skin come off. Place larger chondros in a three-gallon tub, underneath a folded, soaking wet terrycloth towel that doesn't have any fabric softener residue on it. Again, make sure there is very little standing water in the tub, but make sure the towel is saturated and the snake is covered.

Soaking a dried shed off an adult often requires an overnight stay in this setup. I like this method better than using a pillowcase.

Place in a warm area (a rack is ideal), and 24-48 hours later the skin will have come off. Keep the towel over the snake to encourage rubbing. These methods work best when the dry shed is caught early on; really dried on sheds may take even longer soaking, and help from you to peel them off. Be very careful when attempting to help a neonate shed, as they are very fragile. Do not attempt to remove unshed eye caps from chondros; these will come off with the next shed, as will any really stubborn patches of skin. Dry sheds are much more easily prevented than treated!

Swollen Head

Actually, this is not a problem but it can frighten inexperienced keepers the first time they see it. Some chondros experience a swelling of the nose and head during opaque periods prior to shedding. The swelling often persists even after the milky colors clear up, and it can look like a serious problem. The swelling is caused by fluid retention, and will disappear without any further issues once the old skin is sloughed.

Rectal Prolapse

Chondros prolapse part of the bowel each time they defecate; the trouble comes when the bowel fails to retract and becomes swollen, setting up a potentially fatal condition. It is critical to catch a prolapse early, before the tissues dry up and die, or the swelling becomes intense. Prolapse is usually found in the morning, so inspections are important to catching and treating this condition early. If you discover a prolapse, immediately move the specimen to a plastic tub with a shallow amount of clean water in it, just enough to keep the tub floor and the prolapsed tissue wet. Make a thick paste of powdered or granular sugar and water, and apply this paste directly to the swollen tissue, using an eyedropper or a large syringe minus the needle. Most minor cases of prolapse will retract within a few hours or overnight. Those that don't will need to be re-inserted. A veterinarian is the best person to perform this technique, which involves using a blunt probe to push the tissue back in. The tissue may need to be inserted farther than you may think, because the external tissue is inside out, and the outermost part goes back in the farthest. Depending on the nature of the case, some animals may need a "purse string" suture to temporarily keep the bowel from prolapsing again. Withhold food for a couple weeks following the prolapse, and then begin with small meals until normal defecations are observed. Prolapse can be very frightening to those experiencing it for the first time, but most cases are very treatable. It is likely that stress of some kind is the cause of most incidents of prolapse, but dehydration, obesity, or overfeeding may be contributors. It must be emphasized that prolapse can happen to experienced keepers, and animals in ideal environments, and the condition does not necessarily reflect poor husbandry. Animals that repeatedly suffer prolapse may have deeper health issues. Adult females can recover from prolapse and go on to successfully lay eggs if given ample recovery time.

It is critical to keep the swollen tissue moist while waiting for the swelling to subside. Use just enough water to do this, but not so much that the sugar paste washes off. Photo courtesy of Tim Graichen.

Non-Feeders

There are four distinct categories of healthy non-feeding chondros:

Opaque animals, seasonal male fasting, non-established neonates, and unexplained food refusals that do not fit into the first three categories. For help with non-feeding babies, see the section on managing neonates in the previous chapter. Know whom you are buying from. Do not buy hatchlings that have not eaten at least ten times unless you know the breeder well. Opaque chondros usually refuse to eat, and can begin the fast several days before any outward signs are apparent. Seasonal fasting is just a fact of life for those keeping mature male chondros. It usually lasts several months, with no harm caused. The male will resume feeding when he is ready, and will eat what he was used to eating before the fast; in the majority of cases, no fancy tricks are needed. In fact, most of the time these tricks don't work anyway. The male is off feed because his instincts are telling him not to eat, and he hasn't suddenly lost his appetite for rats. The best thing you can do is relax! I offer fasting males food each time I feed the collection, and suddenly one night they resume eating, just as if they had never stopped. Males can go off feed at any time of the year, but most individuals will fast during the same time period each year. When the occasional healthy chondro stops eating for none of the above reasons, there is rarely any reason for alarm, and veteran keepers rarely blink an eye at this, other than to note it. Chondros are sensitive animals, and can go off feed from such a simple thing as being moved to a new cage. Newly acquired animals should always be given a few days to settle in before being offered food. Animals that have been shipped will sometimes refuse food for a while. New husbandry or feeding techniques, a new or different kind of cage… all of these things can bring on a temporary fast. If the snake is healthy, there is no reason to be concerned. They will eat when they are ready. This can be difficult for a new owner to accept, but it is part of chondro keeping. I have found that offering live pre-weaned rats or mice can help in really tough cases, but always use caution when offering live prey. In the great majority of cases, you just need to be patient.

Constipation and Lethargy

I have grouped these together because I feel they are related. How many of us have moved an animal to a new cage, or stripped and cleaned the old one, and had the animal defecate that night? Environmental stimulation is an important ingredient to successful husbandry, and anything we can do to encourage activity is good. Extra spraying, small temperature changes, fresh water and substrate, handling, and different caging can all induce more activity. Many keepers incorrectly think their chondros are constipated at times; older animals have a slower metabolism and often do not defecate frequently. The habit of tail hanging prior to defecation does not necessarily indicate the animal is constipated. If you feel your animal is truly constipated, and is showing distress; if it has a partial defecation and it is obvious there is "more to come"; or if there are fecal smears around the cage from attempts to pass stool unsuccessfully, then some action is needed. The best remedy is a long soak in warm water; this often does the trick alone. It may take several such soakings, combined with gentle handling and manipulation, to cause the bowel to empty. In case of a serious blockage, consult a vet. I have remarked that sometimes the best assurance of getting a defecation from an animal is to clean the cage just prior to important guests arriving to see the collection! Letting the animal crawl on your mother-in-law's white sofa works very well too.

Aggression

Some chondros are quite high-strung, and this must be accepted. However most yearlings and adults will respond to gentle, consistent handling. I do not believe in forcing a chondro that is obviously stressed into submitting to being handled. Some nervous animals will be much more at ease in a large, front opening cage. Smaller cages, and overhead exposure from top opening cages can turn mildly jumpy chondros into biters. Also, keep in mind that females usually undergo a personality change when gravid, but calm females will usually revert to their good-natured selves afterwards. Most babies are snappy, and even those that aren't should not be handled unless necessary. Many chondros will automatically calm down and tolerate handling once they are twelve to eighteen months of age, without any special taming. It must be accepted that a few animals are better left alone as display animals. If personality is very important to you, it is best to buy only tame yearlings or young adults, and do not breed them. If an aggressive chondro in your collection becomes very agitated for some reason, cover the glass or tub front with paper until it settles down again. Chondros can suffer damage from striking their noses against glass.

Respiratory Infection

RI is not uncommon in chondros, and appears to be a common result of the immune system being compromised from stress or parasites, although it can show up for no apparent reason, just as in humans. Symptoms include wheezing or a rattling noise while breathing, and excess mucous in the mouth or nostrils in advanced cases. RI usually responds well to antibiotic therapy. I use a combination of Amakacin and Fortaz, along with subcutaneous injections of sterile water to keep the kidneys flushed, due to Amakacin being potentially harsh to the renal system (see Appendix C). Consult your vet for a treatment regimen that he or she recommends. Mild cases of RI can sometimes be treated successfully by boosting the heat temporarily to the upper 80's or low 90's, with a gradient of course. Seek treatment if the animal worsens, or if it doesn't respond in 48 hours or so. Incidentally, it can be categorically stated that thermally cycling healthy animals for breeding does not cause RI, despite the claims of some.

Mites

Reptile mites originate from other reptiles, not wood or substrate. With proper precautions, it is entirely possible to never have to deal with mites; I have not had a mite in my collection in years. Know that mites *are* present at every reptile show and most pet stores, and act accordingly. If you find mites in your collection, there is just one solution: Provent-A-Mite®, from Pro Products in Mahopac, NY. See Appendix B for the address. I must insist on being firm about this, because for some reason there are a few folks in the herp industry that keep insisting on recommending alternatives to killing mites, instead of using the only product tested and licensed for the purpose. Forget all else; use Provent-A-Mite®, it works, is completely safe when the directions are followed explicitly, has residual killing power, and you will be supporting a fellow herper who has spent thousands of dollars to develop and improve a much-needed product. Mites are not a game or a little nuisance! They can potentially carry deadly disease.

Kidney Stress

This shows up most frequently in neonates that have been stressed from disease or exposed to toxins. It can also result from extreme dehydration or extremely poor environmental conditions. The immune system of neonates is fragile, and the renal system is frequently the first area to show a problem. Symptoms include a dry, wrinkled appearance not related to a dried on shed, and a tendency to retain fluids. Extreme cases can cause the little animal to look like a water balloon, especially in the rear half of the body. As long as the actual cause of the stress is resolved, such animals can often be salvaged. Hydrate them well, making sure to spritz them a couple times daily, and keep meal sizes small, as digesting large meals further taxes the renal system. Incidentally, since switching to Reverse Osmosis filtered water, I have experienced a virtual elimination of this problem.

Skin Disorders

The most common skin problems are abrasions caused from rubbing against part of the cage. These are seen most commonly in the nose and head area. Chondros have a tendency to rub a raw spot on top of the nose or in front of the eyes when they get too active. Make sure there are no rough textured areas in the cage such as screening, on which the snakes can rub. Neonates seem more prone to this than adults, and often rub sore spots on their heads when overactive. Feeding them more frequently can often calm such animals. Move the water bowl away from tub sides so animals can't force their heads in between them. Burns should never occur, because you should never have anything hot enough inside an arboreal cage to injure the animal. The use of heat panels eliminates the risk of burns from heating devices. Fungal attacks are the result of unsanitary cage conditions, or excess wetness in the cage from over misting or inadequate ventilation. If you correct the environmental problems, the skin will usually heal itself with a shed or two, but it may be best to have your vet look at it too.

Spinal Kinks

Although these are not normally a health issue, they often cause concern among keepers, most frequently regarding breeding ability. In my experience, if the kinks are not causing other problems such as nerve damage or bowel movement trouble, then copulation and egg deposition will not be affected. I know of a large female with a horrible kink just in front of the vent that laid large clutches without any problems. By the way, it should be mentioned that kinks are almost always the result of improper handling, and especially from sexing of neonates. Kinks frequently do not show up until the animal matures, but seem to be

This male has a moderate kink at the base of the tail. This type of damage is commonly caused by "popping" babies to determine sex.

more cosmetic than dangerous. However, I did see a Lemon Tree male that was so badly damaged from being "popped" to determine sex that it was unable to move the rear third of its body, and eventually it had to be euthanized following a massive prolapse. Never buy sexed chondros less than one year of age, and don't be fooled by claims that the practitioner has special abilities to perform the procedure without harm.

Grounded Chondros

Some chondros like to lie on the ground at times. This is a normal behavior and there is no reason for alarm if all else appears well… that is, if the animal is coiled normally, is alert, remains active at night, and is feeding. Sick animals look and act sick, but a grounded chondro looks like a healthy animal lying on the ground. Wild-collected animals are frequently found at night crawling on the ground. Most grounded chondros will return to their more normal arboreal habits after a brief time, but a few will decide to make a semi-permanent resting place in some dark corner of the cage, at least during the day. Why? They are just being chondros.

Appendix B. Resources

Listed below are some Internet resources that may be helpful to chondro keepers and breeders. Web sites belonging to persons mentioned in the text are included. Any attempt to make a comprehensive list of personal web sites would certainly fall short, with the potential for offending those inadvertently left out. Therefore, the decision was made to limit the mention of personal web sites to those of individuals that warranted textual reference. No endorsement is made or implied by the author of any of the products or breeders listed here, other than that specifically mentioned in the text; nor is the exclusion of a product or breeder necessarily intended to imply a lack of endorsement of such products or persons. The list is provided as a referential addition to the text for your convenience. All web addresses were current at the time of publication but are subject to change. Product sites are listed first.

Assoc. of Reptile and Amphibian Vets . www.arav.com

Atkins Temptec . . . . www.atkinstech.com
352-378-5555

Habitat Systems . . . . www.habitsys.com
888-909-5795

Helix Controls . . . www.helixcontrols.com
760-726-4464

Pro Products . . . . www.pro-products.com
845 628-8960

Advanced Genetics Wizard . . www.geneticswizard.com

ChondroWeb . . . . www.chondroweb.com

The ChondroForums . . . www.chondroforum.com

Fine Green Tree Pythons . www.chondroweb.com/fineGTPs
(Greg Maxwell)

Lair of the DFTW (Thomas Phillips)	www.chondroweb.com/Lair
Ophiological Services (Eugene Bessette)	www.ophioservices.com
Dr. Guido Westhoff (German site)	www.ophidia.de
Damon Salceies (First albino GTP)	www.kingsnake.com/salceies
Royal Reptiles (Janet Hickner)	www.chondroweb.com/royalreps
On A Limb (Jack Sadovnik)	www.chondroweb.com/onalimb
Signal Herpetoculture (Rico Walder)	www.signalherp.com
All-Chondros (Rob Worrell)	www.allchondros.com
Arboreal Adventures (Buddy Goetzger)	www.arborealadventures.com
Arboreals Plus (Mark Twig)	www.arborealsplus.com
Freek Nuyt (European breeder)	www.fnreptiles.com
VPI (Dave and Tracy Barker)	www.vpi.com

Appendix C. Common Medical Dosages

It is far beyond the scope of this book to diagnose and recommend treatment for reptile diseases. However, the information supplied below may be used by you and your qualified veterinarian as an aid to the dosages of some drugs commonly used to treat the two most frequent chondro maladies: RI and parasites. Thanks to Janet Hickner and Alex Pastuszak for help with this information.

Infections

The most common infection is Upper Respiratory infection, usually abbreviated as "RI" by keepers. Treatment depends on the specific results of doing a culture, but usually empiric treatment is initiated with broad-spectrum antibiotics. I treat most cases of RI with a combination of Amikacin and Ceftazidime (Fortaz®) injected intra-muscular.

Amikacin: (50 mg/ml, 5mg/kl = .1cc/ 1000 gm chondro) This is an initial high dose. Follow the next day with a dose of Fortaz®: (280 mg/ml, 28 mg/kg = .1cc /1000 gm). Give one day off, and then begin a series of injections every three days of both the Fortaz and a maintenance dose of Amikacin (2.5 mg/kg = .05cc/ 1000 gm) until the snake has been given a total of 10 injections of each drug over 30 days. NOTE: Amikacin is hard on the renal system (kidneys) and each injection must be followed with a subcutaneous injection of 5-10 cc sterile fluid such as ringers, using multiple injection sites. Withhold food for the duration of the treatment.

Baytril® is a broad-spectrum antibiotic often used to treat RI and other infections. Great care must be taken to avoid contact with the animal's skin, as this stuff causes tissue necrosis (death) and scarring. Use multiple injection sites to help avoid muscle scarring. Dose: 5-10 mg/kg daily for 10 days.

Internal Parasites

Chondros, especially wild-caught or farm-raised imports, can host a number of worms and other parasites. These two common drugs are considered safe and effective to use:

Panacur® (Fenbendazole) Uses: Removal of Nematodes, strongyloides, pinworms, hookworms, and other macroparasites. Dose: 50-100mg/kg by mouth, repeated in 2 weeks.

Flagyl® (Metronidazol) Uses: Removal of amoebae and flagellates. Dose: 50-75 mg/kg by mouth, repeated in two weeks.

It is important to emphasize that a qualified veterinarian must supervise any diagnosis and drug regimen. The information presented here is intended as a general guide only. There are many medical conditions and treatments that only your vet is qualified to diagnose and treat.

Suggested Reading

One of the motivating factors for the creation of this book is the large gap that exists in the current body of literature. Many technical papers have been presented over the years, and while I find these to be fascinating, some of the content is outdated. All have helped contribute to our current understanding of chondros, and a selection of them is listed here. Some popular GTP articles have been written, and there is a European book about GTPs and Emerald Tree Boas. I have also included a couple titles that have helped me and that I enjoy, that are not specifically about chondros.

Barker, D. G. & T. M. 1994. *Pythons of the World, Volume I, Australia.* The Herpetoculture Library

Barker, D. G. & T. M. 1995. *The Mechanics of Python Reproduction.* The Vivarium, 6 (5): 30-33

Bartlett, R. D. 1994. *Green Tree Pythons.* Reptiles, Vol. 2 (2): 66-69

Blake, H. 1992. *The Green Tree Python (Chondropython viridis).* The Vivarium 3 (5): 19-22

Grace, M. S. & T. K. 2001. *Ontogenic Color Change in Green Tree Pythons.* Reptiles, Vol. 9 (9): 48-54

Guaspari, J. 1985 *I know it when I see it.* AMACOM American Management Association

Kauffeld, C. 1969. *Snakes: The Keeper and the Kept.* Doubleday and Co., Inc. (Reprinted by Krieger Publishing Company)

Kivit, R. & Wiseman, S. 2000. *The Green Tree Python & Emerald Tree Boa.* – Kirschner & Seufer Verlag, Germany

Mierop, L. H. S. van, Walsh, T. & Marcellini, D. L. 1982. *Reproduction of Chondropython viridis.* Zoological Consortium, Inc., 6th Annual Reptile Symposium on Captive Propagation and Husbandry: 265-274

Ross, R. A. & Marzec, G. M. 1990. *The Reproductive Husbandry of Boas and Pythons.* The Institute for Herpetological Research

Switak, K. H. 1995. *The Emerald Serpents of New Guinea, parts 1&2* Reptiles, Vol. 2 (6): 76-99 and Vol. 3 (1): 64-75

Walsh, T. 1977. *Husbandry and Breeding of Chondropython viridis.* National Association for Sound Wildlife Programs, vol. 1 (2): 10-17 (This paper is published on the Fine Green Tree Pythons web site, by permission of the author.)

Walsh, T. 1979. *Further Notes on the Husbandry, Breeding, and Behavior of Chondropython viridis.* Zoological Consortium, Inc., 3rd Annual Reptile Symposium on Captive Propagation and Husbandry: 102-111

Walsh, T. 1994. *Husbandry of Long-Term Captive Populations of Boid Snakes (Epicrates, Corallus, and Chondropython).* Contributions to Herpetology, Vol. 11: 359-362

Walsh, T. 1997 *Life with Green Tree Pythons, parts 1 & 2.* Reptile & Amphibian Magazine, June, 1997 (#48): 14-24

Zulich, A. 1984. *Captive Breeding, Husbandry, and Neonatal Care of the Green Tree Python (Chondropython viridis), with emphasis on the maternal incubation of the eggs.* Zoological Consortium, Inc., 8th Annual Reptile Symposium on Captive Propagation and Husbandry: 114-118

Zulich, A. 1990. *Green Tree Pythons.* Reptile & Amphibian Magazine, Sept./Oct 1990: 2-6